The Tommy Emmanuel Experience

TE CGP

By Dick Ward

I'm in the happiness business!

--Tommy Emmanuel

Copyright© 2013 by Dick Ward

Front cover photo: Juan Junco
Back cover photos: (top) John Watkin
                       (bottom) Juan Junco

All rights reserved. No part of this book may be reproduced in any form or by any mechanical or electronic means, including storage and retrieval systems – except in the case of brief quotations embodied in critical articles or reviews – without permission in writing from the author.

The Tommy Emmanuel Experience
7 $\mathcal{E}$, CGP.

Table of Contents

Foreword. Tommy Emmanuel: First Look

Chapter 1. Elizabethtown: February, 2003 1

Chapter 2. Fur Peace Ranch: June, 2003 19

Chapter 3. Sellersville: July, 2003 27

Chapter 4. Iridium Club: December, 2003 35

Chapter 5. Dual Trip Report: June, 2004 47

Chapter 6. Summer Guitar Frenzy: August, 2004 59

Chapter 7. TE Philosophy 79

Chapter 8. Accelerating Through the Curve 85

Chapter 9. TE in Phoenixville: October, 2004 87

Chapter 10. Epiphany: New Years's Day, 2005 93

Chapter 11. Loren at the RedHouse: January, 2005 99

Chapter 12. FPR with Loren: April, 2005 107

Conclusion 115

Appendix 119

7 ℰ CGP

Foreword

Tommy Emmanuel: First Look

In July of 2002 I had my life-altering introduction to the genius of Tommy Emmanuel. Meeting the man himself came later.

My friend and guitar mentor, Karl Oncken, had gotten me started on my addiction to Chet Atkins and his thumb picking guitar style back in the early 60's. We were in the Air Force, stationed together in Yokota, Japan. Karl convinced me to set aside my little four string Gibson tenor guitar, get a real instrument, and learn what guitar playing was all about. He and I have remained in close touch ever since.

More recently, Karl had been badgering me to go the Chet Atkins Appreciation Society (CAAS) convention that is held every summer in Nashville.

I talked my picking buddy, Loren Barrigar into going with me in 2002. After we got there and settled into the hotel, we met up with Karl and his wife Kei. In going through the program for the week's events, Karl pointed to Tommy Emmanuel's name and said, "He's the one you want to see."

Chet had died the year before and the convention was far less a sad eulogy to the Master than it was a celebration of his life and all he had given to this planet through his music. Loren and I planned to go to the first afternoon Tommy Emmanuel session, which was scheduled to be about 45 minutes long.

Tommy is an Australian guitarist, an icon in his own country. Starting their careers as children he and his brother Phil became, in a way, the Australian version of the Rolling Stones. They traveled about the huge country with their family, musically touching Australians wherever they went. With his guitar Tommy helped open the Sidney Olympics in 2000. As a child he had written a fan letter, which Chet Atkins actually answered, and that started a relationship that was to endure until Chet's death and beyond. I say "beyond" because I have never seen Tommy do a show, a workshop, or basically even have a conversation without mentioning Chet's name.

Loren and I went into the room where Tommy was to perform that afternoon and were astounded by the huge number of people who had chosen to attend. There were several other events scheduled in that time slot, but it seemed like almost everybody had come to see Tommy.

Who was this guy, we wondered and why were there so many people who chose to come for this 45 minute time slot?

We saw many empty seats on the right side of the hall near the front and picked a couple, though the left side was filled up several rows back. That was probably the first item in our CAAS education. You have to realize that this convention draws guitar players from all over the world—over 1500 of them that year. After Tommy started playing, we realized that they were all on the left side of the hall so that they could clearly see his hands. Duh!

In that 45-minute session Tommy mostly talked about Chet. He only played four songs. But those four songs were enough; they changed our lives. We stumbled out of the room and just looked at each other. Neither of us, lifelong guitarists, could have ever imagined such music.

We attended every event on the schedule that week that featured Tommy and some that didn't, where he just sat in with other players. We really did not have language to discuss what we saw him doing, so we just ate, slept and inhaled Tommy's music. Especially memorable were the late night jams in the hotel lobby.

The last night of the convention is always a big concert featuring the many guitarists from around the country and around the world. You have to get in line early to get anywhere near the front of the concert hall. We didn't understand that then, just showing up for the show. We ended up in the about the 68th row of a 70-row layout in a room that accommodates 1200 people. When Tommy's segment came up, he brought the house down with his guitar playing, his energy, his charisma, and his love for the audience.

Following Tommy's part, Loren and I slipped out into the hall for a few minutes to try to clear our spinning heads. A young woman and her mother came out shortly after we did. The woman was red-faced, clutching at her clothing, and fanning her face with her program as though it was unbearably hot. Her mother was attending to her. The poor girl was all a'flutter and it seemed that she was overcome by Tommy's performance. In my many years of attending Tommy Emmanuel concerts, I have witnessed that scene being repeated time and time again.

So began my Tommy Emmanuel saga.

Now let it be known that I am a grown man with a wife, two dogs and a white house in a little upstate New York village. I have five grown children and assorted grandchildren. I play golf and buy my food at the local supermarket and I mow my own lawn. I get a physical every year and am diligent about flossing and making my bed in the morning. In other words, by most people's reckoning, I am part of a pretty low standard deviation of the general population.

With all that in mind, doesn't it seem unlikely that I would up and drop most everything to start following an itinerant guitar player around the country like a durned groupie? But the fact is, I did. The following pages are my attempt to show you why.

7 E CGP

1

Elizabethtown
February 2003

Expectation fervor ran high in the weeks and days prior to the Tommy Fest, a series of weekend concerts and workshops planned for the second week of February in Elizabethtown, Kentucky. I was going to my very first Tommy Emmanuel event that included up-close and personal workshops. It was a chance to meet Tommy and get a sense of the man. I had decided to drive; a new truck, time, and the allure of a road trip were all it took to keep me out of the friendly skies.

Packing road snacks, mucho agua, duds and my new Artist Model Maton acoustic guitar, I headed out from my home in Elbridge, a tiny village west of Syracuse, NY, around 8 am on Thursday the 6th. I drove uneventfully to just south of Columbus, Ohio, stopping for only for bladder relief, and once for gas. At about 4 pm I got a room at a Best Western, got my guitar out and settled in for the night.

Note: To take a look at Tommy's trademark Maton guitar, see the appendix.

About the new guitar, I should note here that after that seminal 45 minutes at CAAS, my eyes had glazed over and I had become the adult guitar-player version of a screaming teenage rock star groupie. I wanted everything Tommy: I had to have the same guitar, the same amp, the same strings, the same thumb pick (those white heavy duty Dunlops), the same guitar strap, and so on. In looking back on it, I am reminded of a high school kid that I tutored for a while back in the 80's. He was an over-the-top Bono fan, (from the Irish rock band, U2). He said, "You don't understand. I don't want to be like Bono; I want to be Bono!" I was not quite that far gone, but I was close, insofar as a feller in his 60's can be.

I started my collection of be-like-Tommy artifacts with a TE guitar strap purchased at that first CAAS convention in 2002. I met Lynn Clapp, owner of Broadway Sound in Knoxville, walking down the hall at the hotel with several of the straps over his shoulder. Broadway Sound does all the sound reinforcement stuff at CAAS. Lynn gave me a strap to look at. They are made of exquisite English saddle leather, with the pieces stitched back to back so that both sides of the strap are smooth. Tooled into the leather is a "C.G.P." in an oval block, a script "*TE*", and a guitar-playing kangaroo. As the strap goes over the shoulder, the words, " Determination" and "Dedication", Tommy's motto, are tooled in on the back.

As I made the decision to buy the strap, Lynn took it back saying, "You don't want that one. There is a mistake in the words on the back." Sure enough

"Determination" was misspelled: "Determinaton". He said that they ran fifty of the straps before catching the typo. Whoa! In between heartbeats, I grabbed the strap back. To be sure, a collector's item! He would not give me a price break on damaged goods though. He said that it was the last of the bad straps; all the rest had been sold. So they are out there folks!

Immediately after getting home from CAAS in 2002, I had called Lynn Clapp at his music store in Knoxville. Tommy plays Maton guitars, exceptionally excellent factory-made instruments made in Australia. At that time Broadway Sound was the only company in the US importing Matons. The exact guitar that Tommy plays is a beat-up Maton EGB808 TE. It is small for an acoustic guitar for the reason that it depends on the pickup system for its sound, not so much the resonation of the body. In other words, to sound good, it must be played through an amp.

It also has a way cool inlay at the 12th fret: "C.G.P." There is a great story behind this inlay. It seems that in his middle-aged years Chet Atkins felt a tad distressed that he did not have an educational degree of any kind. He saw all these politicians and movie stars getting honorary degrees from Harvard and Yale and all, and decided to award himself a degree. From that point on he signed his name, "Chet Atkins, CGP." Standing for "Certified Guitar Player." Chet went on to confer this most prestigious award to only four other players that he deemed worthy: Jerry Reed, John Knowles, Tommy Emmanuel, and Steve Wariner. Some will tell you that the great

French fingerstyle player, Marcel Dadi, received the honor, but others say not. Since Chet's death, the CGP. degree has been retired. Tommy tells me that there are others out there who claim to have received one, but that they are impostors.

Note: Gretsch Guitars says that the title, CGP, was conferred upon Paul Yandell by the Atkins family, after Chet's death.

Lynn said that unfortunately he did not have any EGB808 TE models in stock but he had an EGB808 Artist model that was exactly like Tommy's guitar except for a bit more upscale in appointments than the TE model. He said it was a beautiful instrument and that he guaranteed that I would love it. However, the Artist model does not sport the C.G.P. inlay! What to do? I was torn between waiting to get EXACTLY THE SAME guitar that Tommy plays, or compromising and getting a Maton NOW. I needed it NOW. I had to have it before I went to the Tommy Fest in Elizabethtown in February. It had to be NOW! But it wasn't EXACTLY THE SAME! Arrrrrrrgh!

The tipping point arrived when Lynn told me that if I was unsatisfied for any reason I could always return it. I ordered it; it arrived, and I have been in love with it ever since. Every time Tommy sees it, he picks it up and plays it. Invariably he says, "Lil' Dickie, this is a killah guitah, just a killah guitah!"

Lil' Dickie, you ask? Maybe later. (See appendix.)

I should further note here that I had been called upon to play some music at a memorial service for my dear cousin Kate, who died of ovarian cancer at 54 after a long and intense battle. The service was scheduled for shortly after my return from this trip. I had to play "Let It Be" and "The Long and Winding Road." For some reason I was blocked in my ability to play one passage in the second song, so unfortunately most of my unscheduled guitar playing during this trip was spent working on that stupid passage.

I only had a few more hours to drive to reach Etown so I was in no hurry to get up and get out the next morning. I had planned to play some golf, being ignorant of the Feb. weather in central Kentucky. Wrong again! I got in at about 3 pm and found it to be colder, but with a little less snow, than at home. And I actually had my golf clubs in the truck.

I settled in at the hotel in Elizabethtown, took a nap, had dinner, and decided to get to the concert early for a good seat, since it was general admission. I had driven around town in the afternoon and had gotten my bearings so I was able to go directly to the venue. The John Hardin High School Performing Arts Center was a two-year-old facility, and we are talking state of the art here. I have kicked around high school auditoriums a bit in my time, and they are often a pretty shabby affair. This place was pristine and set up for the "not a bad seat in the house" ethic. The acoustics were splendid. They really did it right. I was to find out later that it is part of a county movement to create an emphasis on the arts. In a cash strapped era when the arts are the first programs to be cut, they made the hard choice to go the other way. Let's give them a big round of applause, and hope that the concept is contagious.

So I got there an hour early for the 7:00 pm show, expecting to help open the place. I was surprised to find myself about 20th in line at the doors. I pretty much had my pick of seats, not counting the first three sponsor rows, which would have been too close for my liking anyway. The seat I chose was about twenty feet from center stage and slightly at the performer's right so as to be able to see his hands clearly. (Loren and I had learned that lesson the hard way in Nashtownville last summer, having excellent seats for all left handed guitar players who took the stage.)

I marked my territory with my coat so that no one would take my seat and explored more of the building. Just beautiful! I also took the opportunity to introduce myself to Eddie D. Mattingly, the promoter of the event. I had had a few email conversations with him on various subjects and he remembered who I was. Meanwhile, the house system was playing Richard Smith music prior to the concert, hyping his upcoming date there. Let it be known that Richard is one of the great fingerstyle players in the world.

People began arriving in earnest at about 6:40 pm and I thought I had wandered into somebody's family reunion. Everybody knew everybody else except me. Etown has a population of about 25,000 but the county surrounding it is huge and replete with suburbia. But these guitar-oriented productions, at the behest of Eddie D.

Mattingly, seem to have drawn a particular set of folks who have come to know each other.

The opening act was a wondrous young player called Michael Kelsey. First of all, he can flat out play, but he has an interesting act to go along with his guitar skills. He has a pretty extensive rack system with all sorts of toys. He did this 10-minute piece where he set up a guitar loop going and then put the guitar down and got shakers and gongs, which he added to the loop. Finally he had what looked like a bass drum head mounted on a ring. He hit that a few times for the loop, and then poured beads into it and made rainstorm sounds. I know, you had to be there, but it was pretty cool.

After interminable sponsor thank-yous by our promoter and host, Eddie D. Mattingly, Tommy came onstage. Remember, I had not yet seen a TE concert in person; other than when Tommy shared his memories of Chet at CAAS the summer before, my only exposure was the Sheldon Hall DVD, a live video of a concert in St. Louis a few years earlier. So I will tell you that I was not prepared for what happened. He put on a show that put the Sheldon Hall DVD to shame! He had the audience from the first and swayed our emotions at his whim. It's like when you see flocks of birds gathering in the fall and when they rise from the ground and swing from one direction to another, the entire flock seems to move as one unit. Somewhere in that flock is the one bird that decides whether to go right or left, or up or down, and the rest move flawlessly with it. That's how it was to be in the audience that night.

The thing about Tommy is that he enjoys his own playing as much as anyone in the audience does. He admitted this in the workshops; he looks forward to playing certain pieces because he "can't wait to hear them himself." You have the feeling that if there were just one person in the theater, he would have put on a show with the same intensity and beauty, just because he loves doing it so much.

He played little that is in the Sheldon Hall DVD. Some songs were from his upcoming album, including a version of "Over the Rainbow" that would make a grizzled roustabout whimper! It was so intense! Otherwise, it was quite a mixed bag; "Avalon", "Who's Sorry Now", and "'Deed I Do", and "Mind␣You␣Own Business", plus Chet medleys, Merle Travis tunes, and some Beatles.

He played for two hours straight. The balcony was empty, but the orchestra was pretty much sold out, which translates to about 400 people. After the show I went out and introduced myself to Tommy's U.S. road manager, Gina Mendello. She is a pretty serious woman. Since I plan to be seeing a lot of her in the coming years, I thought it prudent to make sure she got a load of me. She did and pretty much dismissed me as "one of those." Can't say that I blame her, because I am sure that I was acting like, "one of those." Know this: her duty, as she as she sees it, is to protect Tommy. That she will do; end of story.

I went straight to the hotel because I had a 10 am workshop back at the Hardin PAC. Later I found out that several people jammed for hours in the bar of the hotel while I was languishing in my room, unable to sleep for the excess of excitement from the concert, the anticipation of the workshop, and the funeral music. I wish I had gone out there and met some people at least.

The next morning I did not feel the need to get to the workshop early and rolled in at about 10. To my surprise there were already 15 or so guys lined up in front of the door to the stage where the workshop would take place, obviously planning to get seats up close. They were quite pleased with themselves in direct proportion to their ranking near the door. Then one of those things happened that occasionally makes you think that there is some justice in the world. I noticed a guy who came in just when I did and was filling out a nametag at the sign-in table, so I did the same. The timing was exquisite; Eddie D. Mattingly announced that everyone would need a name tag to be admitted to the workshop area, and as all in line bolted to the table to get their tags, the door to the stage was thrown open and John (the other guy) and I swam upstream through the throng and were first onto the stage where Tommy was warming up. We got seats directly in front and slightly to his right, about five feet from him and he chatted us up a bit. It was sweet!

The workshop was scheduled for 10 am to 2 pm with a lunch break. There were 45 people semi-circled around TE in four tiers; it was too many, but at $90 a head I assume that Eddie D. Mattingly was disinclined to turn anyone away. (By contrast you can get into all three concerts and both workshops this summer in Newport News for $100.)

I will get it out of the way and say that I pretty much held my guitar in my lap for the entire 3 hours and 15 minutes of that workshop. That should be enough to indicate a poor experience, but because it was my first up close and personal exposure to The Man, it did not translate that way. It was very rewarding, I learned a lot, and I got all my prepared and spontaneous questions answered. Suffice to say that he is very specific, secure in his opinions, and willing to share all that he can. I will say that I will probably not pay for another group workshop with that many people in it. For the next one, I will require hands on treatment in a much smaller group. I did however get from this workshop, and the subsequent one, plenty of direction to help me be ready for that more personalized encounter, should it actually materialize. (There are some "guitar camp" type opportunities that restrict participants to under 10 that I will look into when I have progressed to the point that I think I am ready.)

Note: About being ready, please see appendix.

Following the workshop I went back to the hotel, took a nap, met some guys, and did some more practicing for the dreaded memorial service. The passage is not hard, so I don't know why I had so much trouble playing it. Emotional thing, probably.

That night I got to the PAC an hour early to find myself about 200th in line for the general admission seating.

Saturday night brought out droves of people who must either stay home or be otherwise committed on Fridays; back home, I think that a Friday would be pretty much equal to a Saturday draw. I went to the back of the line, resigned to potluck seating. The line stretched down the hall from the entry door to the auditorium and into the school cafeteria. I was familiar with the cafeteria because we had had our lunch there during the workshop. I knew there was another entry door from the cafeteria to the auditorium, and sure enough, a little man stepped out and announced that they would be admitting ticket holders at that entrance also. I quickly sidled over there and was now, magically, 20th in line to enter from stage right. When the doors opened I easily made it to my same seat from the previous night and even saved a seat for another player that I had met during the day. This good fortune in lines that I was having was amazing because it is atypical for me. Usually, I always choose wrong. Go fig.

The auditorium was sold out that night, full of people who knew what was in store. They had either seen Tommy the previous time or had read the reviews. They were ready for a good time and TE did not disappoint. What was most amazing to me was that it was almost a completely different show from the night before! He may have repeated five tunes total! And those were in a different context as he introduced them. I would have been delighted to have had the Friday concert replayed but he didn't even appear to have a set list. He just started in playing and stopped at the end. That simple!

Well not that simple because there was an intermission and he also got a pair of brothers, young guys from Australia who were entertainers, and had idolized TE as young pups, to get up and do a song they had written about their grandmother. Then together they sang, acappella, the traditional Aussy version of "Waltzing Matilda", which sports a totally different melody than the one we are used to. Very nice. Other than that, he just tore the house down with song after song. Some were hot; many were ballads that made you try not to weep. He sang a few things, one a Jerry Reed song, "Today is Mine," that he actually did acappella. It is quite something to experience an auditorium, packed with people, be utterly silent while the only sound is that of one person singing.

Later back at the hotel, a few of us gathered in the lounge and played and sang a bit, but most everybody was heading home Sunday morning and made a short night of it. Not me, of course. I stayed in the lounge until they threw us out at 2 am and was still too hyped up to get right to sleep. Which was unfortunate because I then slept through the Unrequited Jubilant Church of the Ramification service that Tommy played at, and that I had planned to attend. I heard later that he deviated a bit from the Demonstrable Liturgy of the Assumption and got the place jumping. Earlier I had been amused to hear him giving folks directions to the church on Saturday afternoon. He said to go down Poplar Street and turn right at the Catholic Church. The target church was a bit farther down that street. He said, "Don't stop at that first church; those Catholics think they have a monopoly on religion!"

That brought me to the Sunday afternoon workshop. It was held in a very small, no-alcohol, left-over-hippy type coffee house. There were about 20 of us and it was very casual compared to the first workshop. A hot pot of chili was simmering and Tommy was everywhere correcting fingerings, answering questions and suggesting other ways to play things. He played several pieces and spent time with nearly everyone, from the well-established players to the beginners. Tommy wanted to play my new Maton, and I did not get it back for a half hour. "Killah guitah; killah guitah!" Three hours later it was over, though it seemed like an hour, tops.

It is hard to bring the feelings I was left with to the page because they tend to sound sappy. The thing is, though the sessions did not give me anything magical to improve my playing, just being around the guy, just being in the group under the spell he weaves, was so enough, don't you know. I was left feeling that I had experienced the presence of someone special.

I don't know that Tommy will always be able to be this approachable. When he moves to Nashville, his U.S. popularity will grow and it will undoubtedly be harder get as close to the action as I was this weekend.

So anyway, I went back to the hotel and practiced more for the damn funeral and tried to get some sleep during the night. I did not have an early wake up since I was just going up the road to Lexington for the Monday night Woodsongs Old Time Radio Show at The

Kentucky Theater.
http://www.woodsongs.com/webcast1.htm I packed, got on the road and got to heavy-duty horse country by 1 pm. There is some $$$ in that town. Driving in, I passed what I thought were way too many golf courses for one area, but they were horse farms.

The promos said that the doors opened at 6:10 pm for a 7:00 pm show. From the Etown experience I decided to get there pretty early and walked into the theater at 5:15 pm.

The Kentucky Theater is one of those old movie theaters with a huge marquee out front, the kind that have been torn down left and right all over the country. A few towns have the foresight to save them and they are perfect for projects like Woodsongs.

There was no line forming like at John Hardin, so I wandered around the building until I found the actual auditorium. They were doing Tommy's sound check at the time, and down front, amid all the tech people, were Eddie D. Mattingly and his wife, Carol; Gina, Tommy's manager; and Scott Taylor and his wife, Margaret. Scott is a thumbpicker from Lexington whom I met at the workshops.

I wandered down and sort of melded in with that group and sure enough, the establishment assumed that I was part of the TE contingent. So cool! (Yes, I went out later and paid for my ticket; a whole $5!) I got to talking with Scott quite a bit. He is heavily involved with the Kentucky Thumbpickers Club. A very nice guy. He has emailed me a bunch of stuff, like sites to find Chet songs, tabs, programs to download which allow you to slow down phrases while keeping the same pitch, etc.

I am so glad that I decided to spend the extra day and attend the show. It had the same impact that the events of the weekend had. It was a real radio show that they also videotape. But the radio version is syndicated to public radio stations all over the world. They estimate 3.5 million listeners. There were people there telling the audience when to applaud. They gave us the rules before they started taping. It was so much fun. I remember my mother taking me to a Fred Waring radio show when I was a kid and this was just like it. Unlike the laugh tracks of modern times, the producers in that era made the audience a very welcome part of the show. Woodsongs handled us the same way. Very refreshing.

Tommy, of course, was in his usual rare form. He told a couple of those lame jokes from time to time (Piano down a mine shaft: A flat miner/minor), which, coming from his mouth, had the audience rolling on the floor. Michael Johnathon, the host, set up his guitar player, a kid they called "Hot Licks", to have an on-stage lesson from Tommy. He decided to teach him "Classical Gas", at a tempo that no one on the planet could do except him. The kid took it with the good humor that was intended and the audience loved it.

I had purchased Tommy's album, ***Only*** and listened to it a lot on the way home. I was captivated by one song in particular: "Those Who Wait". I listened to it over and over and to me, it was screaming to have words supporting the emotions of the music. Somewhere between Ohio and Pennsylvania I hit gold, I thought with the hook line, "That's how it is for those who wait." Then words began to tumble out: A story about a spouse staying home with the family while her man's far away.

> You know what you'll tell him,
> That everything's fine here
> at home, You'll say what
> you know you should,
> So it's not so hard,
> So you can go on.
>> *Note:*
>> *See appendix for*
>> *full lyrics.*

I had to pull over on the interstate a few times to write stuff down for fear of losing it, something that happens all the time to me. Unless I write it down or record it, be it words or melody/chord progressions, it is gone.

(I had a military deployment theme in mind, though that is not how Tommy heard it. More on that in a coming chapter.)

I had gotten up early and drove 12 hours straight, to get home at 6pm on Tuesday. Very bad driving for the first four hours with many accidents around me, but I managed to cheat death again and got home safely, very excited about finishing my words to Tommy's song.

I was glad to get home to my bride and my dogs but I really enjoyed being off on my own, especially under the circumstances. Eddie D. Mattingly tells me that he will be offering the same fare next year and I may well attend again. Meanwhile I expect to go to CAAS again and to Newport News in July for that three-day event. Just can't stay away, don't you know.

2

Fur Peace Ranch
June 2003

Jorma Kaukonen, (*Jefferson Airplane, Hot Tuna*) owns Fur Peace Ranch Guitar Camp along with his very nice wife, Vanessa. I signed up to go to a session because Tommy Emmanuel was teaching one of the classes. That last sentence is pretty much a summary of my activities from 2003 through 2005, as you will see.

The Fur Peace Ranch is truly at the end of the road. It can be found in the backwoods of southeastern Ohio only if you know where to look. Planning to travel the 545 miles from Syracuse in two days so that I could arrive fresh, I came down I-79, slid past the western edge of Pittsburgh and spent the night just south of Wheeling, WV. I figured I had about two hours left from there and wanted to get in at about 11:00 am, in time for lunch, orientation, with the first workshop at 2:30. My mistake was counting on interstate style drive times all the way to the ranch. Not to be; the closer I got, the lower the speed limit became and the more countrified the roads and the travelers were. I was still an hour out at 40 MPH and so did not arrive until noonish. As the roads and roadlets forked off the last "main road" they got narrower until the last spur led me to a two wheel, rutted track barely wide enough for the truck.

That last road, however, opened to a beautiful meadow in which the ranch was set. Three main buildings were surrounded by the two-person cabins. The main buildings were a kitchen/dining complex (built out of two very old log cabins which were moved to the property for that purpose), a student instruction building with a very small stage and PA system, and the library, a lofted building with the school store and teaching area down stairs and the actual library up in the loft. For more on the library, see the web site:
http://www.furpeaceranch.com/

All three buildings had spacious porches on two sides, with plenty of seating for afternoon and evening picking and bullshitting, of which there was lots. The grounds were beautifully landscaped with flowers, cactus and bushes. Although "Rustic" was the watchword for the overall look, the place was thoughtfully laid out with amenities such as concrete sidewalks connecting the main buildings and no walk longer than 30 yards from a cabin to anywhere else. As an added benefit there was no TV, radio, or newspaper in sight for the entire weekend. I never once encountered the words, "Middle East", which was worth the price of admission alone.

A fourth building has been erected just beyond the cluster of cabins and main buildings. It is Jorma's Fur Peace Station, a new, acoustically designed concert facility seating 180, with a fine PA system. It was there that the Saturday night concert was held; people from the surrounding area come to enjoy the shows. Frequently students from Ohio State, at Columbus, drive in, but they were graduating that week so none showed up.

Jorma himself is a bit on the taciturn side. I don't think he gets too excited very often. Mostly he likes to play acoustic guitar and ride his Harley. He has this huge gold front tooth, which reflects any stray light rays coming at him; it might look sinister were it not for the grin that surrounds it.

Back to my arrival; as I walked in I was warmly greeted by Tommy, sitting on the porch picking, who remembered me from Elizabethtown. I was shown to my cabin and was pleased to discover that I was the only student who had a cabin to himself. That was good, because they are small. The cabin footprint is that of three bunk beds, side by side. Remove the center bunkbed and you have the cabin layout; include a shelf and clothing hooks at the foot end of the bed and room for your dufflebag under the bed. There is a ceiling fan, which is necessary in the hot weather. One note: even though it was hot and humid, there were no predatory insects to bother with. I'm not sure why; no standing water for larva I suppose.

I was not the last to arrive but nearly so; four or five more people showed up. 25 students, all male; 11 for Tommy and the rest were split up between a beginner class and a Delta Blues player. Vanessa, Jorma's wife, conducted the student intake and the orientation. We were made to feel very welcome with a whole list of "do's" and only two "don't's": Smoking only in a designated area (There were zero smokers, students and staff included.) and no drugs or alcohol allowed on the premises.

After that we were introduced to an example of the cuisine we could expect over the weekend. I will not go into detail except to say that some mighty fine victuals came out of that kitchen. They take pride in serving up meals that are discussed with fondness by the students.

Our first class met in the student building with Tommy. He started by playing something elegant and then asked each of us to play so he could get a feel for what level we were at. That request caused eyes to squint all around the room. Here we were with one of the world's best and 10 other unknown players and we were supposed to just "play something." I got pretty nerved up. (We were suppose to be intermediate or above.) However, he started on the other side of the room so I got to play last. That was a mixed blessing, because I found that I was probably about 5th most accomplished out of the 11, but it also gave me plenty of time for nervousness to build. I chose to play my arrangement of "Smile" the Charlie Chaplin tune, and got through it pretty well with complements from TE and other class members. He liked that I had arranged and played a tune "Chet Style" which had not been covered by Chet, as far as we knew. After that he split off the newbies who wanted to learn alternate thumb picking, started them off, and then began working with individuals.

22

Note: It turns out that Chet did record "Smile" in 1973 on the album, ***Alone***. But none of us, including Tommy, remembered hearing the cut.

I will note here that we had three sit down classes the whole time during which he spoke in generalities and gave long detailed explanations on various subjects, i.e. guitar care and set up, restringing (Amazing what there is to be learned there!), keeping steady time, elements involved in arranging instrumentals, his gear and stage set up, and more, and always, Chet, Chet, Chet! The rest of the time he worked one on one with us, guiding us through whatever we were working on, and/or making a cassette tape for which he played a given song through slowly, with relevant commentary. The instruction was informal and very effective, from my standpoint. He was patient and willing to help at whatever level. His credo is that it matters not what level at which you play, just as long as you enjoy playing the instrument.

After supper, we all sat around on the porch and TE sort of "held court" with stories, illustrated with musical interludes, mostly about Chet. We asked lots of questions and had a wonderful time.

The next day's lessons went like the first. Just lots of face time with Tommy. Later in the afternoon, he and Jorma took off to Jorma's studio, a little A-frame off to the side of the property, to work out some stuff to play for the concert. That night, after supper, the 25 students got to watch TE's sound check and he turned that into a teaching situation, explaining about his equipment and how he gets his sound. We were able to claim front row seats for the concert at that time. The house was pretty well filled up by 8:00 and the blues guy, Patrick Sweany opened the show. He was very good, just not my taste though. Then Tommy opened the floodgates. After intermission, Jorma came up and he and TE played several tunes. The concert was over by 10:30. We sat around on the porches afterward until Tommy and Gina, his manager, decided to head to town to get a beer. Some of the guys went with him, but most of us practiced and went to bed.

On Sunday morning, after breakfast, Tommy and I sat in my truck and I played the demo that Loren and I had recorded with lyrics I had written for Tommy's song, "Those Who Wait". This song spoke to me from the first time I heard it on the Sheldon Hall DVD. I had bought Tommy's CD, Only, in Elizabethtown and listened to that tune most of the way back to NY. Half the lyrics were written during that ride. The remainder came hard and took me several weeks to finish. Loren and I got it on tape just before I went to Ohio.

His reaction to the demo was a huge shock to my system. I set it up by telling him that I was so moved by the song, that I had to write lyrics. Truth is that he was quite reluctant to even come with me to listen to it. I now realize that people approach him all the time with stuff like this. But anyway, he was gracious enough to humor me. After the song played through, Tommy sat without speaking. And he sat, and he sat. He sat for more than 30 seconds. Now 30 seconds isn't really that long in most situations, but everything is relative, right?

For me, sitting beside my guitar hero, having him listen to something that I had created as a result of my association with him, well that slowed time down to a tick every 3 years or so. Somewhere in there I guess I snuck a look over at him but he was just staring out the window at the green forest in front of us.

So I'm thinking, "That bad? That presumptuous?" or maybe, "Fairly decent?" or even, "Maybe a little bit good?" When he finally spoke it turned out that it was none of the above. His words were, "Dickie, that hits very close to home." Then for the next half hour he proceeded to explain to me that he and his wife had very recently split up and that my lyrics pretty much nailed the reasons and the rhymes, the whys and the wherefores.

Friends, my most fervent desire at that moment was for the bottom of the truck to open up and for me to be swallowed deep in the bowels of the earth. I wanted to be anywhere at all but in that truck with Tommy Emmanuel.

I was mortified that I had the gall to impose my emotions on Tommy's art. I was stunned that the lyrics that I had written about families being split apart by military deployment, instead took a U-turn and chafed a raw, exposed nerve in Tommy's personal life. I was sure that I had totally blown it and that my tenure as the self-appointed number one TE fan on Planet Earth, was totally and irrevocably over. I fully expected to be banned from concerts and workshops, and to be forced to turn in all my TE CD's. Truly, it was that bad!

But, of course, it wasn't actually that bad. Tommy has contacted me since then and has assured me that he really likes the words. But, sheesh!

On Sunday afternoon, the students put on a concert: well, those brave enough got up and played a song on the student building stage. Jorma ran the PA and all students, teachers, and staff, except Mark, the cook, were present. I fumbled through the tune Loren, Joe and I had written, "Bet You're Gonna Go Far" and, given its humorous lyrical relief, it was a hit.

Everyone who played was encouraged and went away feeling good. Later that day, Vanessa took me aside and explained that she and Jorma are going to produce a compilation CD of student work which will be sold to benefit the Music In Our Schools movement across the country. She asked me to record and send her that song so it could be included; I was quite flattered. It will come out sometime early next year.

We continued working with Tommy through Sunday and after breakfast on Monday, he and Gina headed to Nashville to begin the Three Amigos Tour (it was to be a two week tour with Pete Huttlinger, and Peppino D'Agostino, sponsored by Steve Vai's record label, **Favored Nations**) The students all headed toward home. I drove straight through and got in about 9.5 hours later. I was tired and running on adrenalin fumes.

But--------I can't wait to do it again next year! Back to Jorma Land!

7 ℰ CGP

3

Sellersville
July, 2003

Favored Nations tour

I left Syracuse at 1 pm, headed for Sellersville, PA to see the final show of the Favored Nations Acoustic Guitar Tour. Mapquest had the travel time at 3 hours 45 minutes. That, however, is how a computer sees it, not taking into account the many variables that rear up along the way. One was the stop at Bob MacBlane's shop to pick up some strings and to show him the new Acoustic Xciter pedal from Aphex. Bob is a stringed instrument caregiver and potato flinger (that's, POTATO FLINGER) of some local note. (I suspect you had to be there, on this potato fling thing.) Bob has kept my various guitars in fine mettle for many, many years, and Loren and I enjoy stopping in to see him, even factoring in the bad joke quotient. Therefore I didn't really get out on the interstate until 2 ish. Once in the flow of midday commerce along Interstate 81 south, I made pretty good time, swinging on I 476 to Allentown just before encountering the dreaded black hole of Scranton. (I do not mean to insult Scranton; it is just that is so hard to get through that stretch on I 81.)

Let it be noted that I got lost at Allentown both going there and coming home, ending up at the same Texaco truck stop on I 78-west fer chrisake, both times. I was stubborn the first time, grinding it out with a map on the hood of the pickup. When coming back toward home at 1am though, I gave in without a fight and asked the counter girl to point me toward 476-north. Picture a smirking citizen of the night who has seen it all; she silently handed me a pre-printed slip of paper with terse directions. Before I could stop myself, I had to say, "I guess this happens a lot, eh?" She sighed and moved on to the other customer.

I got into Sellersville at about 6 pm and went behind the theater to where the Three Amigos' bus was parked. I had thought to say hi to Tommy, but Gina let me know none too tactfully that her charges were not to be bothered. I know better than to challenge that fine woman and made just enough small talk to slink away gracefully.

The bus was one from Dolly Parton's rental fleet. A good businesswoman, Tommy says. She has her fingers in a lot of the Nashville commercial pies.

I had hoped to walk around Sellersville and find a place to grab a quick sandwich for dinner but there isn't much of a downtown and I had to drive out to a diner for a turkey club wrap and fries. Actually what downtown there is seems to be centered around the Sellersville Inn and the "Sellersville Theater 1894", so named because during one of the renovations they uncovered a cornerstone with that date which roughly corresponded with what facts were known about the building. It started out as a stable for the inn, but somewhere along the years was converted to a 300-seat theater. They book lots of "out of the entertainment mainstream" acts and lots of children's theater productions. Nice place, well cared for, long and narrow in the style of old movie theaters. Interesting to note that they held the show for 20 minutes to accommodate people who had not finished dinner next door at the Inn.

I was seated eight rows back on the left aisle beside a guy named Dan. We hit it off straightaway and had lots to talk about before the show and at intermission. He was as disappointed as I that the afternoon workshop had been canceled.

Why another workshop you may ask after the recent four days at Fur Peace. Well, I'll tell you; with Tommy Emmanuel it is always something new. Case in point: In the two concerts in Elizabethtown, he repeated maybe six songs on the second night; it was a totally different concert. So it has gone with the workshops. It is always something different and is so intriguing that I can't get enough.

On to the show: Tommy, Pete Huttlinger, and Peppino D'Agostino all took the stage to open the evening. Right from the start it was clear that they were going to be having way too much fun. They said up front that it was the last night of the tour and that no rules applied. I will not be able to name very many of the tunes because of huge synapse gaps in whatever lobe supports that stuff, so I will speak in vague non-specifics. They ripped in to a 12 bar blues invention, which laid the foundation for the evening. Tommy and Pete were quite witty while Peppino was content to be their straight man much of the time. That is until, out of the blue, he deadpanned a hilarious line that seemed to take even himself by surprise.

He left the stage after a few tunes and Pete introduced an instrumental he had written about TE called "Tommy in the Morning" which they played together. All I can remember about it is that I want to learn it. It was wonderful. After a few tunes together, Pete and Tommy gave the stage over to Peppino for his set.

He is amazing. Remaining standing, he positions the guitar so high up on his body that his chin nearly rests on the side of the lower bout. His tone is huge and singular and while he plays a Seagull guitar it sounds like no other steel string I've ever heard. Probably it's a combination of the instrument and technique. He played several original compositions, with lively sections, brooding sections, and heart rendingly beautiful sections, the kind of music that makes tears. And always that tone! He uses his guitar to paint aural pictures for us of the music in his head. A truly remarkable artist. He brought Pete out and they played one tune together before breaking for intermission.

As I was returning to my seat just after intermission, I saw Tommy down front and went down to say hello. He greeted me warmly; you just feel good around that guy. Pete started his set with three unannounced songs. Again I can't remember the titles, but one was a fiddle tune and one was a pop song in fingerstyle. He is a stool sitter.

He then played three more, "Over the Rainbow" which he played to win the U.S. fingerstyle championship in Winfield, and also a Steely Dan song. He is a very technically adept player, fast as hell, yet every note is there, pure and clean. He went on to play and sing "The River is Wide." I really like his voice and his vocal style: true, unadorned and honest. I conjured up Pete as a Civil War soldier singing it, albeit one who could really play the guitar well. If anyone in the theater was unmoved by his performance of that beautiful song they must have been in a coma.

Soon enough, he brought Tommy out; they played one tune together, Pete exited stage left, and the shit hit the fan. Blistering! Several up-tempo numbers just to make it plain that he didn't care how hot a guitar slinger he followed on stage; he came to play! He played several familiar songs from his repertoire. "Michele" was again different than the previous times I heard him play it. It's like that song is organic and mutates every time he puts it under his fingers.

He played for a long time; the show started at 7:40 and he was still going strong at 10:45. There were members of the Delaware Valley Fingerstyle Guitar Association seated at the cabaret tables in the pit. As Tommy ended his set he asked honcho, Joe Willson, what tune he should start his Chet medley with. Joe requested "Mr. Guitar' a song Tommy wrote for Chet. He went on to sample "Avalon", "Lover Come Back", "Wheels", "Windy and Warm", "Trambone" and others.

Tommy then brought Pete and Peppino back and they recklessly launched into "Cannonball Rag", bringing the house down. Tommy and Pete played off each other, while Peppino sort of wandered around looking up at the drops, wondering what all the fuss was about while he played rhythm. Again, I can't remember what all they did for the encore, but it was all unplanned on this last night of the tour, with tunes popping up spontaneously.

Then out of nowhere, Peppino started singing this little pop ditty, which I can't remember for the life of me. I am hoping that Dan will think of it for me. But he just started singing this simple little melody in the face of the furious encore licks that were rippling about and it was in such counterpoint that it was perfect. Tommy, more excited about it than I've ever seen him, and Pete were knocked out and jumped all over it. They pretty much ended with that; there was nowhere else to go.

I had adiosed Dan as the encores began so I could get a head start for my truck and was standing at the back of the theater. As the last note rang through the applause, I bolted for the door, said my goodbye to Gina who was at the merchandise table in the lobby. Zinging with adrenalin, I beat it back toward New York State. Let's not forget my second stop at the Texaco station, but anyway I got home at 4 am, tired and happy.

Tommy always says he found out early in life that when he plays the guitar it makes people happy. Sure works for me.

𝟳 𝓔 CGP

4

Iridium Club
December, 2003

Finally, after several years of threatening to do it, Loren and I scheduled a trip to New York City to see Les Paul. For years he played at Fat Tuesday's and we frequently commented that we should make the trip to see him "before it's too...", well, you know. We were mindful of the pilgrimage that friends Karl Oncken and Jerry Rau made wherein they learned that Les plays every Monday night, unless he doesn't. Unfortunately they picked a Monday that he didn't and, having gotten to the very door of the club before they found out this news, were sorely disappointed. They have decided that it is a trip that they do not want to attempt again. Thus the trip for Loren and me would be partly to avenge Karl's and Jerry's failed attempt and when we learned that Tommy Emmanuel would be sitting in with him on the 29th, it was what, in Syracuse, they call a "no brainer."

Somewhere along the line Les changed his venue to the Iridium Club, which is on Broadway right in the thick of the theater district. It is literally next door to the theater where "Momma Mia" is playing, around the corner from the one showing "Hair Spray", and just down the street from the Ed Sullivan Theater, now owned by David Letterman.

We left Elbridge some time before noon in my truck. My truck, by the way, is really a pickup truck and not an SUV. It always amuses me how SUV owners term the vehicle, "their truck", and yet phone me to bring my pickup to Home Depot to haul anything larger than a breadbox. It does not amuse me that so many SUV owners think that because they have four wheel drive, they are impervious to slippery road conditions. You can tell that they think this because of the way they whiz by you on icy roads. This weekend alone there were three deaths in the area and many fender benders and off the road swerves that can be attributed directly to that delusion.

We headed south on Rt 81, picking up Rt 380 just north of Scranton; this took us to Rt 80 east, which, for the many miles it traces, is really no more than an on ramp for NYC's George Washington Bridge. Our entry to the outskirts of Gotham City and the drive into the actual city itself was simultaneous to the outward surge of all the souls who spend their weekdays there, so we made that part of the drive unscathed by frustration that might have been, had the timing been off. We took a right off the GW bridge onto Riverside Drive, took a left on 52nd St. and pulled into a little open lot about two blocks from the club. After all the horror stories we country boys hear about driving into NYC, it was just that easy.

The sign said that we could park all evening for $8.50, so naturally the guy with the big nose said that it would be $15 for us. We paid it with the understanding that both he and we knew that we were from out of town: end of story. We had to be back at the lot by midnight to get our keys from the attendant before he left for the night and could presumably park there for free for the rest of the night. Yah, right!

As we walked to the club Loren and I had a little disagreement. It was 5:15. The first show started at 8, with seating advertised as "first come, first served". From my previous experience with Tommy Emmanuel events, I maintained that there would already be a line and that if we wanted good seats we would have to get in that line and wait until the doors opened, scheduled for 7:30, according to the website. Loren said that he doubted he would ever wait in line for two hours to see anybody, including St. Peter, and that we should find a place to eat.

When we got there the line was about 12 deep already and, sorry Loren, but we queued up. Loren kept our place while I went to the box office to confirm our tickets. There had been a lot of confusion over the reservations, mostly because I couldn't make anyone at the Iridium believe that I wanted tickets to both shows. Several phone calls, to and fro, over several weeks had been required to sort that out. At the box office our tickets were confirmed by a callow gadfly who assured me that by being thirteenth in line, we would have choice seats and could surely keep them for the second show; Ka-ching: $5 tipsville. Given all the trouble I had already experienced with the Iridium management. I should have smelled a rat right then but instead, relaxed into a surely misguided sense of complacency.

The doors, in fact, opened at 6:30 and we were fairly quickly ushered down a flight of stairs, for the club space is actually underground, by a grumpy man in an ill-fitting sport coat that I thought might be the "Troy" with whom I had wrestled on the phone several times and who claimed to be the club manager. Thinking to remind him of me from our phone bouts, I asked him, nicely I thought, if he was indeed "Troy". He snarled, "Do I look like a 'Troy' to you?" In retrospect, there really is no way that a person who exuded the ill will and downright menace that he did could ever be named "Troy". So, Not-Troy led us to a table for two as far away from the stage as it is possible to get and almost directly behind a large column which cut off the line of sight of the right 50% of the stage. My back was tight to the rear wall and Loren was seated directly in the aisle trafficked by the wait staff. He was bruised and beaten by them throughout the first show. As I said, once I was safely confirmed and thirteenth in line I had let my guard completely down, probably because of thinking that I had prevailed during all the crap I had experienced up to that point. As a result I was powerless to do anything but numbly follow Not-Troy to the outpost he had selected for us.

We too late realized that we were preselected to live at the back tables only by virtue of being a twosome. Had we known this we could have easily formed up with other couples who were in line with us and claimed one of the larger group tables down front. Alas, it is the old story of not knowing what you need to know when you need to know it.

At the table beside us we met a very nice couple, Dave and Wendy Canada, who had never heard of Tommy Emmanuel, having just come to see Les. I primed them to the TE experience they were about to have. They were also taken aback by the seating misfortunes but unlike me, had the wherewithal to do something about it. Wendy was gone for about 15 minutes trying to get better seating. When she came up empty, Dave disappeared for nearly a half hour, presumably working the management for better seats. And damned if he did not get himself and Wendy reseated directly in the center of the house, one seat back from the stage. How he did it I'll never know, but my hat is off to that act of resolve. I think that he must have just willed himself and his wife into those seats. As they left Loren and me back in the Iridium's hinterlands, Dave promised to save seats for us up there in the limelight for the second show.

The first show: Dark stage, dim figures moving out to their places, with someone helping Les to his stool. The house announcer booms out his litany and the lights come up, revealing Les, perched just a little right of center, Lou Pallo, with a black Les Paul on the left, and another guitar player, Frank Vignola, on the right with a, get this, miked acoustic steel string guitar of some kind. It looked like the mike was just an SM 57, nothing special. A grand piano for John Colianni was jammed into the rear of the stage behind Frank with not much room for the guy to even breath. Centered behind Les and Lou was Nikki Parrott, the string bass player. I'll have more to say about her later. I was gratified to realize that there was no lead drummer in attendance, but that's just my tragic flaw revealing itself I expect. So many drummers; so little time.

They played three or four Les songs and then he gave each player a solo song. Needless to say, they were all killer musicians, tasteful, in the groove, and with effortless phrasing like you dream of being able to do. Lou is one hell of a guitarist, comping effortlessly to whatever gets thrown at him and at whatever tempo. Frank, sort of a Django stylist, is one of those players who makes it look too easy; very tasty and understated, but outrageously good. You want to strangle him. John just **was**. What a solid, great player!

Nikki knocked me out. She is a terrific player, doing her job of driving the tempos and holding the bottom, but she has so much more to offer besides. She is a wonderful singer too and a willing foil for Les's gags. On top of that she is gorgeous. She really put style in the show.

The first show is pretty much a blur in my memory because of the convoys of waiters who trekked by, ruining my nice view of the column in front of me, and ricocheting off Loren as they passed.

There were several guests musicians sitting in during both shows, the concept of which is unclear. I do not know how the guests were selected, but it was certainly not because of talent. In the first show, Les welcomed a young guy in his 20's toting a Fender strat to the stage and asked him what he wanted to play. He chose "My Funny Valentine" and proceeded to pluck a dirge-like single string melody line while Les and the band backed him up. I didn't get it then and I don't get it now. Where did this guy come from and how did he get on stage with the great Les Paul with his strat and his funny valentine? Les was kind to him, but did give him some static about, "having the balls to bring a Fender guitar onto his stage."

Les brought Tommy up with fanfare and compliments. He did some of Les's tunes with the band and some of his alone. Nikki, who it turns out is a fellow Aussie, requested that Tommy play Mona Lisa, which brought the audience to utter silence; you coulda heard a microbe drop. The first show started promptly at 8 and ended about 9:15.

With the second show scheduled to start at 10, the house began to clear out and sure enough, Loren and I were able to go down to the seats with Dave and Wendy with no hassle. The table butted into the stage with the stage being the top of the "T" and the table and seats being the leg of the "T". There were about eight seats along each side of the table. Dave saved the first two, on either side of the table for us so we literally could not have gotten any closer to Les without climbing onto the stage. Loren was right at his feet and I was a little to his right, directly below where the guest performers stood. We so have to thank Dave and Wendy for remembering us, because being in those seats really escalated the thrill, especially after our previous seating, and made it the truly memorable night that it turned out to be.

Ok, I'll let it roll for a minute here. I like to think of the second show seating as justice, owed me because of my efforts to get it right the first time. I also like to think that by the time the second show started, Not-Troy had been fired on account of his dreadful sport coat, and had slunk home to his squalid little flat in the basement of a taxi company garage, whining to his ancient cat about how unfair it was that Loren and I had scored the best seats in NYC!

Ok, I admit that is a little harsh, but Not-Troy, just try to be a little nicer to people, ok?

Scott Taylor, a friend from Lexington, Kentucky, and his wife Margaret had come in with Tommy and Gina. Scott came over to where we were sitting and I introduced him to Wendy and Dave; Loren and he had already met. We talked about this and that for most of the intermission.

The second show started like the first, but there was more enthusiasm on the stage and Les was bantering right from the start. He did this little thing with Nikki where he asked her if she wanted to fool around with an old man and she said she would, if she could play with his pacemaker; you can probably write the rest of the gag.

His left hand looked pretty good but his right hand was in tough shape. He held the pick with his thumb and

42

first finger, but his second and third fingers looked to be pretty well swollen and frozen out straight and he made no attempt to use them at all. He did, however, occasionally pick the high E string with his pinky. The notes and expression were still there but the speed was gone. But he played far past his physical limitations, to the extent that the audience heard all the Les licks that they expected, just from the suggestions he played. It was remarkable.

Les's guitar was tricked up with who-knows-what gadgets; there were knobs and switches all over the thing. He had four or five interconnected stomp boxes at his feet and on a mike stand just to his left was a little black box with a few knobs and switches. But with all the variables of knobbing and switching and stomping that he had at his disposal, the only thing I ever saw him touch was one knob on the mike stand box, which often he would readjust before starting a song.

His body may be 88 years old but his mind was as sharp as ever and he cracked wise just like the old days. There were more guests during this set, one an Asian or maybe Eskimo woman with a wonderful voice and style, who had been there a couple of weeks prior as a guest and, as a result, was doing a New Year's Eve gig with Nikki. A large black preacher man moaned the blues real good, but I could have done without his wife following him on stage to sing.

One fun thing that happened was that when the preacher was on, Les was talking to him about playing with Ray

Charles. Les started laughing and asked Loren to hand him up his glasses, which were down by the stomp boxes. It turned out they were dark glasses and he put them on and started the Ray Charles bob and weave with his head. Hmm. Guess you had to be there.

Then Tommy came back on.

It was interesting to see the homage that Tommy paid to Les by choosing tunes and setting him up for solos. He would do the foundation work, establishing the song with the audience, and then pass it to Les for him to shine on. A wonderful thing to watch. Les was just as even handed, praising Tommy and insisting that he play his own stuff so he could watch. Once after Tommy had played something hot, he asked Les what he wanted to play next. Les said, "After that? Do you think I'm crazy? Well, after that I'm not going to play a damn thing!"

There was much more energy in the second show and Les played a lot more, probably stimulated by the exchanges with Tommy. It was still going strong at 11:45 when Loren remembered that we had to go back to the lot and get the keys for the truck. He was kind enough to run back on his own and was back in a few minutes, just as the show was ending. Les and the band left the stage and Les looked very tired and had to be helped off. The musicians must have split right away because we never saw them again. The announcer said that Les would be out to sign autographs in 20 minutes, and we were to make a line starting where the waiter was holding up the towel. Loren had had enough of lines though so we mingled and stood around. Finally, 20 minutes later, we got in line but I started to worry about the truck being there without an attendant so we decided not to wait for Les, but to hit the five-hour road home. That turned out to be an excellent move because Scott tells me that Les did not come out until well after 1am. I had brought some artifacts for Les to sign for Karl and Jerry, and because Scott was planning to stay to the bitter end anyway, he was kind enough to get them autographed for me.

I know I have left a lot out but it was overwhelming and I wasn't taking notes. The trip home was uneventful though, the best kind. Loren got us out of the city and into Pennsylvania, and then I pushed us on home. As always, we rode the final fifty miles on Ronnie Milsap's, ***Stranger Things Have Happened*** album (arguably the best modern country album in existence, just ahead of George Jones', ***Cold Hard Truth***.) We rolled in at 5 am, exhausted and glad of it.

5

Dual Trip Report:
June 2004

The Birchmere, June 11   Hugh's Room, June 17

President Reagan's funeral was scheduled for June 11th, the same day Bruce and I were going to the Birchmere in Arlington to see Tommy Emmanuel and Martin Taylor. While we thought we might have caught a break because all government offices were shut down, suggesting less Friday afternoon traffic, we did not know if it meant that there would be congestion because of the services, what with those wishing to pay their respects and the inevitable rubberneckers looking for some cool funeral action. It turned out to be mostly a moot point, thanks to the sorry state of affairs in what passes for travel on the roads of Penn's Woods. In midstate PA on Rt. 81, we encountered a seven-mile stretch of stop and go and mostly stop, which took about an hour and a half. When we got to the actual point where the problem was we could not tell if it was construction or an accident. Anyway, clean up of something was happening and because both southbound lanes were closed, traffic was being routed **through** a rest stop. So, by the time they finally got there, travelers did not know whether to piss or pass.

Bruce Wood, a fellow golfer and neighbor (about a 3 iron away), is a fine guitar player. He has studied the instrument for many years and has the discipline to play at least a little every (read: <u>every</u>) day. He has studied flamenco guitar, having gone to Spain to buy an instrument and take lessons. More recently he is working on the Latin rhythms of Jobim, etc., sambas and bossa novas and the like. I will forever be in awe of the fact that when he wishes to learn a new song, he simply obtains the sheet music and learns it from strange little squiggly marks on the paper. How do you do that?

We wanted to be at the Birchmere well before 5 pm. because the box office opens then for ticket pickup. My experience with Tommy Emmanuel concerts dictated that there would be a substantial line when it opened so we wanted to be there early. But because of the Pennsylvania effect, there was no chance. When we got to the decision point at the beltway, we were programmed to take the western swing. At last gasp however, I thought I saw one of those temporary signs proclaiming that traffic on 495 west would be experiencing significant delays so I had Bruce abort the 495 west flight plan and divert east instead. Naturally, the second we were committed to take the east route. traffic slowed to a stop. I swear I heard a subtle chortle from the direction of Hanover, MD.

(Ok; that Hanover, MD thing is a little inside joke. While I was stationed at Yokota, Japan in the USAF during the middle 60's, my guitar mentor, Karl Oncken, and I played in a country band and would travel around the area to play in Officers' and Enlisted Men's clubs. Getting somewhere on time in Japan in those days was always a challenge. There was so much roadwork being done that even the construction sites were under construction. Trying to guess the best way to get from point A to point B in the shortest time became a source of great amusement, because no matter which way you went, it was always the longest way.)

But I digress. Here is how it works at the Birchmere: At 5 pm the box office opens and you pick up your tickets. First in line at that time gets a line number. When the doors open at 6, that number is the first called and first allowed into the room to choose a seat, and followed by succeeding line numbers. The line numbers are little slips of paper, dispensed from one of those machines that are intended to maintain order in the push and shove, "Me first!" world of delicatessens, bakerys, and dry cleaning establishments. Our grade school lessons of good citizenship and taking your turn are mysteriously abandoned in situations like these; we instead tend to revel in our efforts to stealthily imbed ourselves in the service line in front the little old lady who has been waiting patiently since dawn and the poor widow with five grimy children. Thus are these machines, invented by nuns, put into place so that we have to take our number, and, doing without the illicit thrill of beating out our fellow humans, glumly wait our turn.

The first in line at 5 does not get number "1"; instead it is merely the number where the machine left off from the day before. That seems unfair, doesn't it; I mean after conniving to be first in line and then getting number "004274" is disconcerting. But none the less that is the first one that will be called. When Bruce and I finally got to the box office at around 5:45, we got a line number that was about forty down from the starting point for the day. We did not think that was going to be too bad, in terms of getting good seats in a 250-seat room. Wrong again. It turned out that the line number represented group transactions as well as the normal two-ticket sales. So it was that, as the line numbers were called out at 6, we watched over a hundred people troop in ahead of us. When we finally got in, all the up-front, close to up-front, nearly up-front and even semi up-front seats were clearly taken or saved. I had Bruce stake out the first hinterland table that was available while I cruised up toward the bandstand in a pathetic search for two unclaimed spots.

In a situation like this, asking if an "empty chair" is a "taken chair" is rather like asking the flight crew on a doomed airplane if they might happen to have an extra parachute. The question is met with a barely suppressed sneer. As you make your way through the front section, actual vocalization becomes unnecessary. You make eye contact with the person nearest the empty seat, then glance down at the seat itself and then back at the person, while elevating your eyebrows. They hold your gaze for a moment, taking pleasure in giving you false hope and then dash your expectations with an almost imperceptible headshake and/or inverted smile reflex. This look clearly says, "You shoulda gotten in line sooner, you sap!"

As I made my way through this futile exercise I came to the point where, in order to maintain any shred of dignity you stop asking people and just make like you are walking to or from the excellent seat you won by being in line extra early. So as I was walking back to the table Bruce was holding in the rear of the room, I don't know why I stopped at a table for 4 and asked the couple seated there if the remaining two chairs were taken. But when they told me to help myself I had to ask again. It was literally the best table in the room. About 18 feet from the direct center of the bandstand, it was back just far enough for perfect viewing and, as it turned out, listening. So thanks to Frank and Marianne Gurley, the worry about seating that had been plaguing me since central PA, was a fool's exercise. But who knew?

Martin Taylor is an elegant player and gentleman. As the concert started, on time by the way, he came on stage wearing a buttoned-up woolen suit jacket, a riggin' that I would find confining to play in. His program was one of mostly standards, rendered in his inimitable style of three distinct parts: bass with the naked thumb, harmony rhythms and single string lead lines. His technique with the thumb is unique in my experience in that he picks up and down as one would with a plectrum. His other fingers are totally independent of the thumb and of each other. It is rubbing the head and patting the belly, taken to the extreme. Jazz drummers have that kind of independence with four limbs, but it is rare to see in a guitarist. In addition to the standards, he played one "novelty number." Well it was a novelty in its set up alone because once he got to the meat of the tune it was pure Martin Taylor talent. He threaded a piece of paper about the size of a dollar bill under and over his strings just in front of the bridge. He told us that he had been bored in his hotel room while on a tour in Africa and came up with a musical invention. He began to demonstrate five separate rhythmic motifs of a few notes each. Each was unremarkable and suggestive of nothing in particular but he played them for us, separately, a few times to imbed them in our minds. Then, one at a time he began to combine them. The end result was an intricate melody easily identifiable as of African inspiration, with, because of the paper insert, a steel drum flavor. After playing it through, he wound it down, removing parts one at a time until only the original motif remained. It was amazing and certainly a showcase for his astounding talent.

After a short intermission, Tommy came on and opened with "I Go To Rio"; up-tempo del mucho! A great opening tune with a memorable intro hook. From there he spiraled into his thing, with emphasis on songs from the new album, ***Endless Road***. It was his usual high energy, "Stay with me because I offer you no other choice," performance. He grabbed the audience from the start and had his way with them, as usual.

He has a new twist this year. I have mentioned his beautiful young traveling companion I believe. I first noticed her last year at The Chet Atkins Appreciation Society convention in Nashville when I thought she was somebody's daughter. Well, I am sure she is, but I mean daughter of a friend of Tommy's. I was disabused of that notion a few weeks later. I continued to be stupid at the Newport News Tommy Fest and thought that she might live in that area and had traveled with parents to Nashville. I actually had occasion to speak to her during the day when we both stood at the rear of the Yoder Barn as a workshop wound down. She was obviously waiting for Tommy. Thinking to make small talk, I asked her if she were the chauffeur. She chuckled and said, "Yeah. That's me, the chauffeur." When I saw them together playing kissy face the next day at the theater on the Jersey shore, I realized what a dundering fool I had been.

Anyway, Tommy has added her to the act. Her name is Liz Watkins and she is a terrific singer. He brought her up to do three tunes with him. She started with the Dolly Parton/Chet duet, "Do I Ever Cross Your Mind". Next was the Momma Cass tune, "Dream a Little Dream of Me", and then she sang and played with Tommy a song she wrote for her deceased uncle. Let me tell you, this gal can sell a song! She was completely at home on stage and was foil to some of Tommy's antics. She won the audience right from the start and they loved her by the end of her segment. Tommy referred to her as his "better half"; go fig.

Tommy did several more songs and, I suspect, used up some of the time meant for Martin Taylor to join him in a finale. MT came back on and they did two standards together. Other than absolute world class guitar work that meshed like they had been rehearsing for weeks, the only notable side bar was when Tommy blurted out that "At home in Scotland, 'Marty' actually lives in a castle." Martin got about two inches from Tommy's face and politely requested that he not call him "Marty". They may have come back for an encore; I misremember.

We had most affable and interesting tablemates in Frank and Marianne and struck up the type of TE event friendship that has become the norm in my travels to his concerts. We have been in touch since and may see each other at future concerts. Nice people.

I did not mention this to Bruce because I did not wish to dilute his enjoyment of the concert, but at the time I thought that Tommy was a little "off." I had experienced that once before in afternoon and evening concerts at the Surflite Theater on the Jersey Shore. That booking was on the Monday following the 2003 three day Tommy Fest in Newport News. There was a Sunday night concert and then an all night drive to New Jersey. I had the same drive but I got some sleep before leaving; they did not. That afternoon and evening, the fatigue was evident. Similarly, at the Birchmere, I thought Tommy was a bit tired, but unless you had seen him play as much as I have recently, you would never suspect that.

The trip out of the area on Interstate 495 commenced at around midnight and was uneventful. We drove back toward Baltimore and after we had swung to the west we found a hotel, Hampton Inn, I think, very nice, and slept until 8 am or so. We rolled into Elbridge on Saturday with no further excitement, and no excitement is good at this point in a road trip.

The following Thursday, my bride and I left at midmorning for the four-hour drive to Toronto. Tommy was booked at Hugh's Room and Carol had never seen him in person. The journey north was smooth and we checked into the hotel in the mid afternoon. It was a very nice hotel for a very nice price. Carol had done some Priceline.com prospecting and got us a pretty good deal for downtown Toronto. We were to meet friends from Hamilton, Ontario at the club for dinner and the show. They also had never seen Tommy. We walked around the city for a while and then got ready to leave for the evening. There was a subway stop literally under our hotel and we were able to get to within two blocks of the club that way.

We met Trish and Peter at the club and were led to what proved to be a great table. I was still smarting from my seating debacle at the first Les Paul show at the Iridium, in New York City, and had specified a table right up front at the band stand in my reservation arrangements at Hugh's. As the host led us to a table on a level about 4 feet above the main floor and about half way back in the room I reacted with "Here we go again" body language. Our seating dude assured me that not only was it the best table in the house to view a performance, but that upon hearing that I was coming to the show, he had set it aside especially for me. I thought, "Arrrrgh; Not-Troy has had a hand in this!" I reasoned that my seating challenge issues must have preceded me, even to a foreign country. Resigned to being, yet again, dissed by the seating gods, I put up very little fight, but lo and behold, it indeed turned out to be an excellent vantage point.

Our meal was clearly fine dining, leisurely and delicious. We had arrived about 7 pm and the show was scheduled to begin at 8:30. We had time to enjoy the dinner and conversation, catching up on happenings with our friends. Hugh's Room seats around 180 diners, I would say, and all seats offer excellent concert viewing. The sound system was quite adequate and competently managed. In all, a great place for one's first exposure to The Man.

The opening act was a local folksinger. He was very good and obviously a regular performer at the venue. His style and material were Gordon Lightfootish, much of it written himself, and though not at all what I am currently interested in, a pleasant way to pass the time until the main event.

And when the main event finally arrived at around 9:15, there was standing room only; it was like the roof was a-tremble. Tommy took the stage by storm, again starting with "Rio", and wearing, for the first time in my experience, a jazzman's suit jacket, ala Martin Taylor. That did not last long as it was already a bit warm in the room and the frenetic energy of his opening numbers soon forced him to frock down to his usual open-necked shirt.

If Tommy was a little "off" at the Birchmere, he was most certainly in the "ON" zone that night at Hugh's Room. He played pretty much the same program but from the start he drove the audience at his whim. About 20% of the audience had an idea what to expect from him, but the rest were taken by surprise. When he gets a ratio like that he really plays to it and takes them wherever and however he chooses. It is really something to see. He brought Liz up in the second set and she did the same three numbers and was warmly received.

Tommy closed the night with a medley of Chet tunes and was reluctantly allowed to leave the stage with a raucous standing "O". Our friends had a long drive back to Hamilton and left shortly before the show ended. I wanted Carol to meet Tommy so we hung around after the show. Gina clued me in to where he would be doing the meet and greet so I was able to get us almost at the front of the line. I introduced Carol to him and after a brief chat, we headed for the subway to go back to the hotel. As she turned away, he caught my eye and nodded at her, giving me a winking "thumbs up." Great judge of talent, that lad!

On Saturday, we puttered around Toronto for the morning and headed to Hamilton, spending the night with Peter and Trish. We drove back to Elbridge on Sunday.

Whew.

6

Summer Guitar Frenzy
2004

It was July. I had just gotten back from CAAS, fer cryin' out loud. So what? Here's what! More Tommy. Bring it on.

CAAS was about the same as it had been the first two times. I was getting to know Tommy by then and he greeted me warmly whenever he saw me, but at the convention I just watched his shows. I stayed away from him in the hotel halls and "meet-and-greets" because he is in such demand that the poor guy gets no rest unless he's locked up in his room. He clearly did not need me monopolizing any of his time. Also, I knew that I would be seeing plenty of him down the road.

"Summer Guitar Frenzy" would be the longest guitar related trip to date, consuming 10 days, three music venues, six states, mucho air miles and a 14-hour marathon homeward leg through four airports. It also revealed a look at the really ugly side of airport baggage handling

I was able to enroll in the Accent on Music Guitar Seminar in Portland, Oregon by filling one of the last two available slots, one of which opened when a guy from Singapore, who had attended a previous AOM seminar, was denied a visa. Sad what our terror-ridden world has come to. The seminar, hosted by West Coast guitar educator, Mark Hanson, featured Tommy Emmanuel and John Knowles, two of the four CGP's in the world. TE needs no introduction but John, while being a household name in fingerstyle guitar circles, is not as well known by the general public. Which is its loss; he was Chet's right hand man for 30 years. With a PhD in physics and bright prospects for a career with Texas Instruments in the early days of electronics sub-miniaturization, he chose music instead and we are all the richer because of it. He is an elegant player, a teacher of the first rank, and a most pleasant gentleman to hang out with. Should his music career ever flag, there is always standup comedy as a sure-fire back up

TE was also doing the Tommy Fest East in Newport News again with Stephen Bennett, which immediately preceded the Portland seminar, so I decided to attend both and make a tour of it.

I had been having trouble with pinched nerves in my wrists and left elbow, which affected the strength in my left hand such that I was unable to play my Maton steel string guitar. Fortunately I had my wonderful and very excellent new Sand nylon string at hand and would have to take that with me. I ordered the guitar from Kirk Sand at the CAAS convention in Nashville right after my friend Karl ordered his in 2003. His was serial number 439, making mine number 440. I could not resist the temptation and had David Church make a gold nameplate that proclaims the instrument to be "A 440, " referring to the universal tuning frequency. David incidentally is the artist who is responsible for crafting my idea of the "river of gold" fret marker system that Kirk inlaid in the fingerboard.

Note: See a picture of **A 440** in the appendix

Taking the Sand immediately presented a problem in that the Maton, while dearly loved, is replaceable while the Sand is not and I worried about flying it across the country. I had had no trouble in transporting guitars in the past using the "carry on" system, thus avoiding the trash compacter which is the airport baggage handling machine. A guitar fits nicely in an overhead compartment and I had purchased a backpack hard case cover to facilitate the walks from arrival gate to departure gate. But you never know. That indeed turned out to be the truth, as we will see. I just never knew.

I had an early flight out of Syracuse to Charlotte with a commuter turboprop connecting flight on to Newport News. You have to actually walk out on the concrete to get on these little connecting flights so as I approached the turboprop, my guitar case was taken from me, red tagged and I watched it carefully placed in the baggage compartment. These little airplanes have smaller overhead compartments so there is no option to carry on a guitar. But, no problem; they handled it with extreme care. Remember this happy little episode for I will be referring back to it.

I arrived in Newport News and took a cab to the Hampton Inn on Jefferson Avenue. It is just up the street from the Yoder Barn and is not so coincidently also owned by the Yoder family. As it turns out the Yoders own a slice of just about everything in the area, including the large Patrick Henry Mall. Seems that entire strip along Jefferson Avenue used to be pastureland for the Yoder dairy cows. The Hampton Inn is reasonably priced, clean and comfortable and very well managed. It offers a very nice continental breakfast every morning, and 3 days later, when I was up and in the lobby at 4:00 am, waiting for a cab to the airport for my 5:30 flight to Portland, to my delighted surprise a member of the morning staff was already on duty and had a brown bag breakfast ready to hand to me as I went out the door. Now, c'mon; you gotta be impressed by that!

I got into my room at about 2 pm in the afternoon and immediately took a swim. When I ordered my tickets in March, the staff at the Yoder Barn had told me that the hotel was within walking distance of the concert venue. My afternoon investigation proved that to be a bit of a stretch, for it is about a mile away, a concrete mile of intense heat and humidity by upstate New York standards. However the hotel shuttle driver was happily willing to run me down there at about 4:30 that afternoon. I ate in a KFC near the Yoder Barn and wandered over there 5ish. Previous experience has taught me that when there is general admission to a TE concert, you better be there early if you want a good seat. So I was the first one there. I have a particular seat in the barn that I covet and I wanted to be sure of getting it. In fact I was there so early that the folks who sell cut flowers during the day in the entrance building were still set up for business. I chatted with them and with Christine Yoder and others and helped them load unsold flowers back into their van. So it happened that while others were lining up in the heat outside, I was in the comfort of the lobby acting like I naturally belonged there.

When the general public was allowed in to join me in line at the doors to the theater area, I thought that the second person in line looked familiar. It turned out to be Mark, the very excellent chef at Jorma Kaukonen's Fur Peace Ranch, and his wife Ellen. We had a great time talking about Fur Peace stuff while waiting to be let into the theater and I learned that TE would indeed be back at Fur Peace in April of '05. Yippee!

This year Tommy Fest East consisted of three concerts and two workshops. The previous year it had been two and one. The following year it would become four and three. Nothing succeeds like success.

The concert opened with a young player from Australia who was traveling with Tommy just as Clive Carroll did last year. Simon Bruce is a nineteen-year-old singer/songwriter who is very talented in a Paul Simon sort of way, though he sports a bit of a smoldering nonchalance in his presentation on stage.

Following Simon's 20-minute set of ballads, Stephen Bennett took over. God, I love everything about this guy's show. He is so calm and laid back on stage that he ought to have a pacemaker for safety-first considerations. The music, composition, style, technique, and everything else you can think of is just wonderful. I could sit in his audience for hours and hours. He played several songs from his new album, ***Everything Under The Sun***, as well as many other selections. I just grooved through the whole set and grinned in anticipation of the Saturday and Sunday sets as well. Frequently, like TE, he does quite different sets on succeeding nights. Unfortunately that would prove to be misplaced anticipation.

Tommy was warmly received and, as usual, played his ass off. He gets so turned on by an audience that I worry that he may fly up into the air someday. The only down side of the set was that the sound guy had the front end speakers placed differently this year such that they nearly blasted me out of my favorite seat. It was not a problem with Simon or Stephen, but TE ratcheted the sound pressure up a notch or six, as he will do, and it was just too much. I decided that I better retreat to my second favorite seat for the remaining concerts. Again, that would be moot by the next morning.

I spoke to several people I had met the year before and got to know some new folks. We milled around for a while after the concert and business was brisk at the merchandise tables. Finally Grant and Sheila, whom I had met the year before while standing in line to get in, gave me a ride back to the hotel. Before going to bed I had to play a little didn't I? I was pretty wired and picked for 20 minutes or so and then cashed it in for the night.

I remember waking up during the night on my back and being short of breath, basically gasping for air. I think it is a sleep apnea thing I have recently developed and probably will go away as I continue to lose weight. Anyway, I woke up in the morning feeling lousy and immediately realized that I was in A-fib.

If you don't know, atrial fibrillation is a common, non-life threatening heart condition where one of the upper chambers of your heart gets out of its rhythm and just flutters. Frequently it is accompanied by an elevated heart rate, which can be alarming. I am on a medication to control the racing heart rate part of it, but the irregular beating makes me feel really crappy when it happens. In my case, it is not symptomatic of a sick heart; just one that is confused about when and how often it should beat. The only danger is involved with not treating it in a timely fashion to get it back into rhythm. If you let it go, the blood in that chamber can stagnate and clot, putting you at risk for stroke. So you need to get to a hospital within the first several hours and have it put right.

I have experienced it six times now over the last five years and when it happens I just go to the hospital and someone from my cardiologist's group comes in as says, "Oh, you again", zaps me with the defibrillator, and I'm on my way home in just a few hours. As I am sure you have intuited by now, that was not how it was to be in Newport News.

I am not going to tell the whole sordid story here; suffice to say that they were ultra conservative in their treatment of this big old Yankee boy who wanted only to be hooked up, jolted, and sent out the door, thank you very much, and "See ya!" I went into the hospital Saturday morning, and did not get out until middle afternoon on Sunday. By then I had missed the Saturday workshops, the Saturday night concert, and 90% of the Sunday workshops. I went to the Yoder barn for the last hour of Stephen Bennett's presentation. After that I went back to the hotel. I had to be at the airport at 4:30 Monday morning. I was so absolutely exhausted, not by the heart thing, but by being in the damn hospital, that I decided I had to skip the Sunday concert and get some sleep instead. I had a big sirloin at the Steak Back Outhouse, as Tommy calls it, and went back to my room, packed, and passed out. I did not pout too long about missing all the action because I still had a week with Tommy, John Knowles, and Mark Hanson to look forward to, but I am sorry that I missed the workshop time that I intended to spend with Stephen Bennett this year. I hope to be able to work with him at next year's event, or perhaps at another venue.

Note: To see a nice gesture from Christine Yoder, manager of the Yoder Barn, regarding my brief illness, see appendix.

At the airport on Monday morning, I was set for a repeat carry-on performance on my shuttle flight to Atlanta.

Sure enough, like on the ride out of Charlotte, they took my guitar, red tagged it and carefully put it in the baggage hold. I was flying Delta this time and had had a very good guitar carry-on experience with them when I went to Aruba in January with the Ithaca Ageless Jazz Band. So I was not unduly alarmed when, after landing in Atlanta, I climbed off the shuttle jet to see a baggage conveyor belt snugged up to the cargo hold door. My alarm factor did escalate rapidly though when I stood by the wing and watched suitcases being ejected from the hole in the plane and landing on the moving belt. I watched six bags fly out of the compartment. I know because I was unconsciously counting them. My last rational thought was, "Why aren't they hand-carrying my red tagged guitar case over to me?" The seventh item to take flight out of the hold was mine. I watched in horror as my precious new Sand guitar was thrown out of the hatch and bounced off the conveyor, plummeting five feet down to the cement!

Passengers are not allowed to pass the rear of the wing while they wait for their carry-on baggage–federal regulation. So it is a miracle that I am not in a cell in Guantanamo Bay, being held for prosecution under some aspect of the Homeland Security Act. I went ballistic, rushing toward my guitar and was gently, sort of, ushered back to the regulated passenger area. After things calmed down, I insisted on opening the case and inspecting the guitar in front of the boss baggage handler. Though the case had a nice dent in it, the guitar seemed to be OK. Because a guitar is a box made of rather thin pieces of wood, all subject to integral stress and tension, I worried about the equivalent of the summer road stone chipping the windshield and then watching in winter as the crack slowly traverses the glass. So far though, nothing has shown up.

When I got to Portland, I went to the baggage department and made a detailed report on the incident involving my guitar, so as to create a paper trail, should there be problems with the instrument in the future. It was there that the nice lady told me that under no circumstances would the Delta gate employees allow a guitar to be carried on any departing Delta flights. It seems that no guitar carry-ons is a Delta policy that is not well enforced, except at the Portland airport. I had had no trouble carrying a guitar on Delta flights to and from Aruba and no trouble going to Portland. Nice Lady convinced me, however, that I would be checking it on my outbound leg, period.

Going home I had my two itineraries to complete: Portland to Atlanta to Newport News and then, Newport News to Philly to Syracuse. If you noticed, that is four airport trash compacters in tandem, a formidable gauntlet for A 440 to brave. I knew that the odds of its survival were slim so I accepted the inevitable and had a "Clam" overnighted to Portland. The Clam is a coffin like corrugated plastic container, which suspends a guitar case in foam brackets and offers the most protection for a guitar that I have seen to date. CaseXtreme in San Diego makes it. **http://www.casextreme.com** It cost as much to overnight it to Portland as it did to purchase it, but from the standpoint of insuring safe passage for my poor guitar, it was well worth it. With that decision made and out of the way, I was able to settle back and enjoy the prospect of five straight days of immersion in guitar heaven.

There were 30 of us enrolled in the seminar, which blatantly figures out at ten players per teacher. But through the miracle of creative scheduling and seminar experience, Mark and his wife Greta were able to get the teacher-pupil ratio down to six to one. Think of it; a world acclaimed player/teacher and six of us supplicants. A daily schedule started with a master class presented by one of the three teachers. The rest of the day was broken up into five 50 minute periods; a given student had one period with each teacher and five other students, and two study halls, which were free periods given over to self-directed activities, including practicing, rewriting notes, jamming, napping, or taking one of the auxiliary classes with Greta. In seeing the schedule, my initial thought was, "Hey, what is this? I am paying all this money but I am with these teachers for less than four hours a day!" My second take on the subject, after a couple days of classes was, "Hey, what is this? I'm trying to absorb so much here that I'm exhausted, and also really need more time to practice!"

I will not attempt to break down the content of individual classes or to generalize about the lesson plans of the instructors; suffice to say that just about every conceivable aspect of fingerstyle guitar playing was addressed, from technique, arranging, dynamics and breakdown of specific tunes, to writing, performance, storytelling, guitar care, and, threaded throughout, humor. Questions were enthusiastically encouraged and copiously answered.

One interesting note on John Knowles' style is to be found in his working motto. He strives to, "...be a better teacher than most guitar players and a better guitar player than most teachers."

We were sequestered on the beautiful wooded campus of Lewis and Clark College. (Indeed, the week we were there, Tommy, much taken by the beauty of the general area and stunned by the magnitude of the trek the two explorers endured, wrote his beautiful song, "Lewis and Clark".) We lived in one of the student dorms, directly across the street from the building that housed the cafeteria and the rooms we used for classes. Though there was some grumbling about the cafeteria food, personally I thought that it was varied and generally pretty decent, and that anyway, the complaints sounded a bit forced and obligatory, harkening back to universal high school cafeteria expectations. All I know is that, as in my days as a public school teacher, I went into the cafeteria hungry, and came out not hungry. What more can you ask?

We all quickly got to know each other and there was soon plenty of jamming. There was always a night session where several of us gathered in the dorm lounge, sent someone on a beer run, did some playing and some BS-ing. My buddy, Geoff Richard from Virginia, quickly established himself as a force to be reckoned with, spouting all manner of lies, and usually left us with sore bellies from so much laughing. That man will say whatever is on his mind, don't you know.

Thursday and Friday evenings were reserved for student recitals in the group instruction room. Participation was optional though most of us chose to perform. As a class we played at levels that fanned across the ability spectrum. But no matter what level we played at, we were all as nervous as hell, and were all warmly received and acclaimed by our peers. Most of us played a three-song set, some just instrumentals, and some with vocals. Some of us felt we needed an accompanist for one or more of our songs and had to make do with the likes of John, Tommy or Mark. When you are desperate you will take anyone. The recitals went very well and it was a great way to spend an evening. I was the final act in the Thursday night session. I chose to play my arrangement of the Japanese folk song, "Hamabe No Uta" ("Song of the Beach"). This is a beautiful melody that Karl Oncken taught me while we were stationed at Yokota, Japan in the early 60's. As an interesting side bar, Chet toured the Far East in 1965, heard the song, and subsequently recorded it on an album, ***Discover Japan***, which was never released in the US.

After that solo, I invited Tommy to join me for my other two songs. He seamlessly followed me as I used chop sticks from the cafeteria as props on my novelty take off, "Just a Closer Wok with Thee", and my old standby, "Alice and Pearl", a song that I wrote somewhere in the early 70's. Once we got started, I was having so much fun that I forgot to be nervous. The others seemed to like it and for me, it was a great way to close the evening.

On Saturday night the three teachers scheduled a concert that was open to the public. It was held in an old church that is used as a concert venue. Fortunately seats down front were reserved for the students because it was flat sold out to Standing Room Only. The doors were to open at 7:30 pm and by 6:45 the line was well down the street. This is remarkable because Tommy had never played in Portland, and John was a relatively unknown performer. So either they came to see Mark play, or they trusted his concert track record enough to not want to miss it. Or maybe the word about Tommy Emmanuel is getting around.

Mark opened with a 20-minute set of the music that he so tastefully writes and/or arranges and so gracefully plays. He and John then collaborated by way of segue into John's set. John Knowles is an elegant player: he plays a beautiful classical guitar with a minimum of effort and a maximum of feel. His set flew by and made me yearn for more.

After intermission, Tommy took over, sporting his new stage look: Patent leather shoes, $800 Italian suit, buffed, trimmed, and squared up and ready to take the stage at Carnegie Hall. Left over from his old look was confidence and enthusiasm, both just popping out of him, and a palpable eagerness to hear his own music himself, as well as to share it with the sold out auditorium. This was his first performance in the Portland area and you could tell that he was bent on leaving an impression; on giving them something they had never experienced before and would talk about and remember after he was gone. Let me assure you, he did just that.

Many of the AOM students had never been to a TE concert, and even though they had just spent a week with him, did not have any idea of what was coming. I struck up a conversation with some Portland folks seated behind me, Tom Dearborn and his wife, who I think were expecting something like a heartfelt "leftover hippy" type singer/songwriter. I gave them my usual pre-Tommy pitch. You see, part of my pleasure in a Tommy concert is setting up newbies and enjoying their reaction. In the vernacular, they were "blown away". Tommy did rock Portland that night. He always gives 100% in concert, but when he is playing an area for the first time, he seems to develop a heightened pace on stage, to pick up a momentum roll that takes him over the top. And when he is astride that steed, he grabs the audience and pulls them with him, deep into the extraordinary. What a night!

I must also mention Tommy's partner, Liz Watkins. She always comes on and does a few songs with him. She is a wonderful singer and has a polished a stage presence. She is an enjoyable and welcome addition to his shows.

From the seminar in Portland, I took two major lessons away with me that would have made the trip worthwhile even if they had they been the only rewards. First, I have always fought tension in my hands while I play. I assumed that it came from nervousness. John Knowles quietly pointed out that I was using my hands to try to do two things at once: Play the guitar, and hold the guitar. He showed me a position in which to place the guitar such that I no longer had to support the guitar with my hands and rather, could let them float across the neck of the instrument as I played. Well (expletive deleted), but oh my; what instantaneous improvement was wrought. As I have continued to work on his suggestions, my playing has become more and more fluid and tension free.

Secondly, though I have played for the public since I was a teen, I have a history of intense nervousness while performing. Tension builds in my hands and throat and I have trouble playing and singing freely. For some reason this is exacerbated by playing with or in front of other guitar players; so where am I going, trying to play with John, Tommy or Mark in the room? Two things happened to me in Portland that have markedly changed that situation for the better. First I became aware that pretty much all of the other players there had the same problem in varying degrees, so why am I making it into such a big deal; secondly, I took Greta's performance class on performance anxiety. Now some of the things we covered in the class were not huge revelations to me, and some were, but for some reason, Greta's presentation I expect, I guess I internalized them that time and they "took". When I went up to play for everyone, the tension and nervousness were pushed way back under my excitement and the high I was on from the fun I was having.

This is what happened in Greta's performance anxiety class: There was Greta, three students, and a video tape machine. Each student was to introduce and play a song while Greta video taped it. When the song was done, Greta asked the player to self-critique the performance. Then each of the other students talked about it, and finally, Greta gave her opinion. The wrap up was an open discussion among the four of us about the performance and how to deal with the stage fright.

When my turn came, I did a song that I wrote, one of my favorites, actually. I have done it for years and know it perfectly. And with an audience of three, don't you know I screwed up the words in the second verse. I stumbled and tried to cover it up with spontaneous lyric writing, and managed to get through the rest of the song without slitting my wrists.

When it was time for my self-critique, I focused on the second verse gaff, severely castigating myself for being so stupid. I never even looked for anything that I did right, instead focusing on the negatives of having made the mistake.

When Greta asked the other students what they thought, the first one said, "Mistake? What mistake; I didn't hear any mistake!" The second said, "Yeah, I heard that part but I thought it was suppose to be part of the song. I thought, well, he wrote the song; he must know how it goes."

I was flabbergasted! They hadn't even really noticed. When Greta's turn came, she said, "Yes I heard the mistake, but the song is so beautiful, that it didn't really matter."

Friends, I knew that this was a huge learning opportunity and I took it. It helped me develop a whole new perspective on performing music.

I came away from Greta's class with a three part approach to solving performance problems: Identify what the problem is; create a solution; and then, practice the solution like you practice your guitar licks. For example, I would find that I stopped breathing while playing demanding guitar lines. As soon as I "practiced breathing" during the line, with as much emphasis as I would practice the fingering or the dynamics, the problem began to recede.

Since then, I have done one concert back home here at a library, just before my wrist surgery, and experienced only low level nerves, which I think is normal and can be turned around and used for good vibes in the gig. When I hear the recording of my AOM recital, I can hear none of the tension symptoms in my voice or hands. I feel I have passed a huge milestone in this.

In packing to leave, I was so grateful to be able to put my beautiful A 440 in the Clam and not give it another thought until I unpacked it at home. The trip from Portland to Atlanta, to Newport News, to Philly, to Syracuse was long and tiring and blessedly uneventful.

Well, except for this: On my way home, while waiting to board the shuttle from Newport News to Philly, I watched the incoming baggage being unloaded from my plane by one overworked female baggage handler. She was short and round, and had to get a running start to hitch herself up and into the baggage compartment. So once she was in there, the floor is still five feet above the concrete surface of the taxi area. And she is working alone. And she had to run and jump up, so there is no baggage cart or platform in front of the baggage hatch. You guessed it; she had to drop the luggage out of the hatch down to the concrete. She tried to drop the bags softly, don't you know. After five or six bags got dropped out, she dropped out. She dropped out on top of them, climbed down, and carried them over to the baggage cart train. Then she ran and jumped and started over.

Later, on my way out to the airplane, I mentioned it to the gate attendant. Well, "mentioned" might be a bit light, but anyway the best he could come up with was that they were short-handed. I took his name and everything, but never did anything about it. You get weary. I did tell the pretty young flight attendant about it though while we were on our way to Philly. I told her what I had seen and that I was a lawyer. I said that I had a guitar in the back of the plane and that I would be watching while it was unloaded. I said that if I saw anything remotely like that happening to my guitar, I would go home and initiate a class action lawsuit on behalf of anyone who had had baggage damaged by Delta over the last 10 years. She listened politely, made the requisite "cooing" sounds, and smiled reassuringly, basically just waiting until I was done so that she could get back to work. I felt better though.

I was glad to be home to my bride and my dogs. I made several new friends, as always on these guitar trips, and plan to correspond with them indefinitely. Getting together with those from the West, as I do with my East Coast guitar buddies, however, will be more problematic. But who can tell? Times, they are a'changin'.

Note: For the trip itinerary for "Summer Guitar Frenzy" see appendix.

7

TE Philosophy

An email I wrote to fellow participants of the Accent On Music seminar in Portland, OR, shortly after getting home:

Hello all,

I don't know about you but I have found it hard to come down from our week. Of course since it took me four airports and 14 hours to actually get back down on the ground, coming down from an experience has taken on a whole new literal meaning.

Many of you asked me about my previous experiences with Tommy and particularly about Jorma Kaukonen's guitar camp, Fur Peace Ranch, so I thought I would break it down for you all.

I first saw, no, experienced Tommy (You don't "see" TE, you "experience" him, as you all now know.) at the Chet convention in Nashville in the summer of 2002. Since then, I have been to another convention, several concerts, workshop weekends, and now two extended guitar camps. I had to be talked down off the ledge by

my bride, or I would have traipsed off to Ireland, and
followed him around there too! I even thought about
using the excuse of having recently found long lost
relatives in Australia, which really happened to me, to
go there as well. Geoff Richard once said that he
wanted to get all of Tommy he could because, at the rate
he goes, Tommy may burn out at some point. I took that
to heart. I now know that it is very unlikely that he will
burn out; this is just the way he is.

Since that first encounter my life has changed
profoundly; I guess that, because of Tommy Emmanuel,
I have had a rebirth----a musical and behavioral rebirth,
not religious, but I think I may understand the "born
again" religious concept a little better now because of it.

This man's playing, attitude, work ethic, life philosophy,
and so forth, have swept over me in the two years I have
know about him, and as I have come to actually know
him. I have rid myself of much of the extra stuff in my
life, both possessions and obligations of time, distilling
it down so that I am concentrating and spending my
hours only on the things that are most important to me.
This can sound sappy when I say it to some, but you
people know exactly what I am talking about. As a
result, I have been practicing for a minimum 1 hour per
day, and usually more, for over a year and a half.
Amazing what that will do for your chops!

I have totally stopped playing in bars where alcohol and
conversation can make the musician a barely tolerable
background distraction. I put together a tidy little PA
system and I do two set gigs in local libraries and coffee

houses. I play for the 15 to 30 people who have come solely to hear my music. When I am done they tell me how much they enjoyed it and ask when and where I am playing again. They seem happy to have been at my show and that, now, is what makes me happy.

I am also going "on tour" in the future. Here's how I envision that: In my Tommy travels, I have made many friends who love the kind of music that I do. I plan to set up tours as I drive around visiting them. For example, in Richmond, Geoff Richard will get a few of his guitar and music lovers together at his house or some other place where we can meet for free. Geoff will play a short set to start the evening and then I will do a set, after which we will do a couple tunes together and an encore (presuming the thunderous ovation). I will have come from my buddy Neal Walter's place in Pennsylvania before that. I'll continue on a circuit of stops like that for a couple of weeks or so. As I teach guitar here at home and am a teacher by trade, I will include a fingerstyle workshop. Low overhead, no club owner hassles, no hauling equipment home from a smoky bar at 3 am; just playing my music for people who want to come and hear it. All I need is a place to stay and maybe a meal or two. Sound good?

As I have said before, in most non-Tommy ways, I am a fairly normal person, a retired teacher with 5 grown children and several grandchildren. I have a nice home in a little country town in upstate New York with a wonderful wife and two dogs. I have always had many varied interests, being a sort of jack of all trades, master ...well you know the rest. But since my TE encounters, I have changed. I have realized that at 62, I want to sharpen my focus, concentrating only on the 3 things that are really important to me, and letting the res go. After family, those are guitar, golf, and I enjoy working with wood in my basement shop. I am a pretty good golfer by general standards. I shot two-over-par on my last round, and have always been an obsessed golf addict, like some people I'm sure you know. But tell you that if I had to choose, I would drop golf in favor of guitar in the proverbial heartbeat. Tommy had to make that choice with tennis. He always enjoyed playing, but it began to cause tendonitis and he turned his back on it instantly.

Do I expect to play 300 nights a year like TE does? Of course not, but I have taken the inspiration from him, knowing that he walks the walk to back up the talk, to reevaluate my goals and myself. And I tell you that I am loving the little movie of my life that I see playing out in front of me in the years to come.

The above I got from Tommy; I haven't even begun to think about what I will internalize from John Knowles. Scary thought, huh? I think I will start with what he said when he saw somebody using one of those capos that attaches with a couple layers of bungee cords wrapped around the neck, "I see you believe in safety first with that enriched capo there."

I will send my experiences at Fur Peace Ranch by separate email.

I had a wonderful week with you all and am so glad to have met you.

Dick Ward

𝟳 𝓔 CGP

8

Accelerating Through the Curve

I became a real guitar junky during these years from 2002 to 2005. Just so you don't think I am keeping anything from you, I traveled to every Tommy-related event or camp that I could manage without breeding a divorce. In an effort to prevent myself from droning on, as I can be prone to do, I will touch on some of the interim events without giving you the blow-by-blow.

My first visit to the Chet Atkins Appreciation Society was in 2002 with Loren, and we have attended every year since then. However the scope of this book is 2002 through 2005. You already know about the first visit; the events in the other CAAS trips have been pretty much the same. Drive or fly to Nashtownville, check in to the Music City Sheraton, meet up with old friends, go to the Bar-B-Cutie for lunch and dinner, and wallow in fingerstyle guitar until you stumble back to your room in the wee hours and try to flush your adrenalin overload so that you can do it all over again the next day.

I followed Tommy to Newport News, Virginia, in 2003, 2004 and 2005. These events were hosted by Stephen Bennett. He is a fine guitarist, known for resurrecting the harp guitar, an instrument he found in the family attic. It had belonged to his great-grandfather. He is also a great guy and I have come to know and love him over the years. The format for this event in 2003 was a Friday night concert with Stephen and Tommy. Then Saturday workshops, morning and afternoon, and a Saturday night concert.

In 2004, the format changed to a Friday night concert, workshops on Saturday and a concert that night. Then more workshops on Sunday and a final concert on Sunday night.

In 2005, it went to a four-day rotation. Do you sense a pattern here? Right! Nothing succeeds like success. I know that must be true because I read it in a book.

Finally, I went to my second Fur Peace Ranch weekend in 2004. It was very much like the first, enjoyable entertaining, gastronomically sensational, and instructional in every respect. They really treat you well there! The biggest difference between 2003 and 2004 was out on the porch when Geoff Richard told the joke about the ant and the elephant. It was so funny that we nearly had to call 911. It involved a monkey in a tree and a coconut that was used as a guided missile. Geoff finds himself quite entertaining. If you put him in a round room and tell him to sit in the corner, he will be happy for hours.

Now back to the in-depth folderol.

𝟳 𝓔 CGP

9

TE in Phoenixville
October, 2004

After a summer of nothing but guitars, guitar related travel, and a little golf here and there, it was only fitting that I round out my fall with a road trip to a Tommy Emmanuel concert. Just seemed like the thing to do. He was on an East coast swing and would be in the tiny little burg of Phoenixville, PA, just east of Philadelphia. I was lucky enough to be able to double my pleasure by including a stop in Greencastle, PA to reconnect with old friends, Neal and Coleen Walters; well not that they are actually so old, but I mean I've known them—never mind.

Neal and Coleen are seasoned musicians, working with another couple in the Old Time Music band, ***Doofus***. **http://www.doofusmusic.com** Neal has developed a top-drawer digital studio in his home and does well, recording and producing CDs for other musicians. Of course he still has nearly every bit of analog equipment he ever owned too, but the new digital stuff is really impressive. Neal is a packrat. The walls of the lower floor of his house are lined with shelving that display thousands of CDs, DVDs, records, cassettes, reel-to-reel tapes, videotapes and books—probably even some Edison Phonograph cylinders around too. It is a vast repository of media. Most, if not all, of his collection is recorded into his high-end computer. He frequently sets the whole collection on random play and it will jump from one end of the spectrum to the other, allowing him to be reminded of albums he may not have heard in years. I find that very cool.

I am also quite interested in another facet of Neal and Coleen's lives. They go on tour. They actually plan a circuit of what they call "house concerts" at the homes of friends and acquaintances that they have met in their Old Time Music circles. This tour is usually in conjunction with a festival they have been invited to play at somewhere and the house concerts are scheduled along a looping route to and from the festival. They have the roadies, themselves of course, pack up the van with their equipment (They do not carry a PA, preferring to play "au naturale", but Neal uses several instruments and Coleen plays a dog house bass.) and off they go, reveling in a vagabond life of the touring musician. They usually are on the road two to three weeks, sometimes more.

The house concerts are often augmented with workshops and private lessons. They charge minimal amounts for ticketing to these events, trying to make just enough to break even on the expenses of the tour. I am very interested in this concept as an outlet for my own performance aspirations. I think if my hosts were willing to do a little legwork, I would try to expand the concert location possibilities to include local libraries or other similar venues where a small audience could be accommodated.

I think I have mentioned this concept to a few of you and while you have been able to curb your initial enthusiasm, I have high hopes that your fervor is dawning and that I will be able to put together a tour sometime in the not too distant future.

After spending Wednesday evening and much of Thursday with Neal and Coleen and really enjoying the new twig and foliage diet they are both on, I set out for Phoenixville and the TE concert. Neal and Coleen were planning to meet me there later in the evening after I had secured good seats by virtue of my early bird predilections. Again, as in Sellersville, the venue was a reclaimed theater from the early 1900's. Much care has gone into restoration and the work continues. I love it when a community does this. So many of those old theaters have been torn down to make room for a distant section of a Wal-Mart parking lot that never has any cars parked in it. Progress, don't you know.

Naturally, I got there very early and Tommy was in the lobby, having just arrived for sound check. I got to go in and be there for the sound check. He had his new Sand guitar (not the Richard Smith model, but the other, thin one), which is so beautiful, and with such a pure, Chet-like sound. He played "To B or not to B" for me to demonstrate the new axe and it was so good. After the sound check he suggested that I put my guitar (can't leave it out there in the pickup, now can I?) in his dressing room and come to dinner with them. I put the guitar back there, but declined the dinner invite, needing to stay at the theater to meet Neal and to hold the seats. However, a serendipitous confluence of two events allowed me to take him up on his offer after all. Dan Sarm, a friend I had met at the Sellersville concert, and whom I was also holding seats for, arrived and agreed to stand watch over our prime location while I went to dinner (five rows back and on the left; five rows back to be within the optimal cone of the throw of the PA speakers, and on the left so as to be able to clearly see TE's left hand work (For those of you taking notes, reverse that position for concerts involving left-handed guitar players.). Then, on my way through the lobby, Neal and Coleen came in, having been held up at home and not having had dinner yet either. So the three of us went to the restaurant and got a table right beside Tommy. I was able to discuss the idea of a TE concert in Syracuse with Gina and him, making that concept one step closer to reality.

The show was terrific. As always the newbies in the house came away gasping, after being taken quite unaware by what they were to experience. Liz brought out a new song she had written about her siblings called, "That's What Brothers and Sisters Do." Also her mom was in attendance, so when she did the tune about her uncle, who died young and unexpectedly, there was a poignant moment for all.

After the show Dan, Neal and Coleen and I said our goodbyes, and I saddled up, intending to drive north until the buzz of the evening wore off and then find lodging. I had very explicit directions out of Phoenixville to a route that would take me to Interstate 476N, and a straight run home. Neal had printed out a detailed map and it looked easy. Well guess what; I wandered around southern Pennsylvania for a while, that's what. I should have known what was coming when I couldn't even get out of Phoenixville on Route 113 without getting lost and ending up on a spooky one lane trail that ended at "The Reservoir". It was a perfect setting for an alien abduction, a thought that occurred to me as I was standing outside the truck taking a leak.

I backtracked all the way to the theater, found where I had missed Rt. 113 the first time, and was again on my way. A half hour later though, 113 sort of petered out with no more route markings. Young scamps probably had removed the signs. 113 must have turned somewhere that I didn't because I ended up at a convenience store in some little locality that I never noticed what it was named. A reasonably articulate employee told me that from where I was, to where I wanted to be, I should just as well back track on 402S to 76E, head toward Philly and pick up 476N near King of Prussia, PA. Why didn't I think of that? It didn't work out that way, of course and I found myself on 76W for a while. It was Ok though, because I have always yearned to have a legitimate reason to mention "King of Prussia" in correspondence.

I finally got to Interstate 476 and drove well past Allentown, nearly to Wilkes Barre and found a Comfort

Inn at 1:30ish . I slept 'till 7:15 and then drove back into Elbridge by noon.

I survived my first carpal tunnel procedure in September and it has been pronounced a success. Guitar withdrawal was annoying, but I have been getting back into playing during the past week and it is so fulfilling. But don't rejoice too much on my behalf, because I get to have the other wrist done on Monday and will go back to admiring how nice my guitar looks hanging there on the wall. Before the first operation one of my fine friends actually said, "Look, I know it is just a routine medical procedure, but just in case something goes wrong during the operation, can I have your Sand guitar?" With friends like that...

My sights are set on going to the Fur Peace Ranch guitar camp in April with Loren. Only five months of central New York winter to negotiate. Why, spring will be here before you know it! (Groan)

𝟕 𝓔 CGP

10

Epiphany
New Year's Day, 2005

After following Tommy all over the country, and after considering trips to Ireland and other foreign lands to stay on his trail, I had a resounding epiphany. Why keep traveling so much? Why not let Tommy do the traveling for me? After all, that is who he is, guitar player, traveler, Roadmaster; why not ask him to come to me for a change? Written down, it sounds like I was presuming a lot. But I reasoned, that since I am affiliated with an organization of over 100 guitar players located in central New York, would they alone not be the seeds for an entirely new Tommy Emmanuel audience? After seeing a concert, would they not tell everyone, "You gotta see this guy!" In a year or two would we not have a growing audience base, to ensure Tommy's return year after year?

Well friends, that is exactly how it worked it out. It happened this way.

After the 2004 workshop with Tommy at Fur Peace

Ranch, Loren started doing something that I had never seen him do before. He began to practice. He began to practice like a crazy man. You need to know why that came as a shock to me.

I first met Loren when he was in eighth grade. A middle school teacher in central New York, I stepped out of my classroom on the last day of school before Christmas. The teacher in the neighboring room was standing in the hall shaking his head. Bill Durham (We called him "Bull" of course) told me that he had brought his guitar into school that day to play some Christmas songs for his class. He had played a while, and one of the kids said, "Mr. Durham, why don't you let Loren try." Bill told me that he had never seen anything like it. I stepped into the room and saw Loren playing like no 14 year old should ever be able to!

At that point I did not know all the "Loren Lore": that he had picked up one of his dad's guitars at four years old and lugged it into the kitchen where his parents were sitting. That he had told his father that he wanted to play "In the Mood" with him, and that his dad could play rhythm, but he would play lead. And then just did it. At four years old.

I did not know that at 6 years old, he is, to this day, the youngest person to ever play at the Grand Old Opry stage; That he was Jim Ed Brown's guest and blazed his way through "Yackety Ax" on a Gretch Country Gentleman guitar bigger than he was.

I did not know that he had studied guitar with Jimmy

Atkins, Chet's big brother and member of the Les Paul Trio.

All I knew was that this kid could play! I got to know him and his family. He and I began to jam from time to time, and I went to their shows. As he grew older, out of school, our friendship got stronger and became what it is today.

The thing is this: In all those years that we played together, hung out together and traveled around together, Loren never practiced. He just picked it up his electric guitar and went to the gig. But now, after seeing Tommy that first time at CAAS, it seemed like he was never without an acoustic guitar in his hands. Even in his sleep. You think I am exaggerating, but it is true. Loren often fell sleep on the couch with his ax, watching a Tommy Emmanuel video, or listening to a CD. The music would loop over and over while he slept. When he woke up he was able to play the licks.

You will remember our road trip to the Iridium club to see the Les Paul. As we headed to NYC, we talked about Tommy, and the concept of solo acoustic guitar shows. Later, Loren was dozing as we rolled by Wilkes Barre, PA on Rt. 81. Out of nowhere he stirred and said, "Dickie, nobody wants to hear me play guitar." It gives me chills to think about that now.

That brings us back to 2005. In January, Loren had his first solo acoustic guitar show in a new 90 seat venue in Syracuse, the RedHouse. He was much in demand as a sideman for other musicians, or with his own band with his brothers, but this was his first solo show. I think we packed 130 people in that little place and they put to rest for all time the notion that nobody wanted to hear Loren play guitar.

Meanwhile I was busy learning how to be concert promoter. With help from three people, Jim Horsman, owner of a local events production company, Tommy's manager, Gina, and Steve Dahl, Tommy's booking agent, I scheduled our first Tommy Emmanuel concert in central New York for April, right after Fur Peace. What a rube I was! I knew nothing about the process, and without the help of those fine folks, it would have never been anything but a wish and a joke. But when the dust settled we had managed to plan back-to-back shows for one evening at the little RedHouse theater. More about that later.

In April of that spring, Loren and I went to the Fur Peace Ranch seminar with Tommy. Loren began to come into his own on that weekend, and he and Tommy worked out a couple tunes to play together at the RedHouse shows: "Borsalino" and "Cannonball Rag" (That trip is when we met the Kiwi dude!)

So in July, for TE at the RedHouse, Loren, Jim and I beat the bushes for people to buy tickets. Aunts, uncles, neighbors, acquaintances, co-workers, you name it. Nobody in this area had heard of Tommy and all we had to work with was Loren's budding solo acoustic guitar reputation and our slogan, "You gotta see this guy!"

Lo and behold when show time arrived, we packed the

90-seat place with 130 people for each show. People were hanging off the rafters! If the fire marshal had known, he would have gone ballistic!

I don't know if you have ever experienced this, but when you have a packed in, sold out horde of humanity for an event and the place starts to literally heat up, the crowd seems to take on a life of its own. People feed off each other's excitement, almost exponentially. That is how it was at the RedHouse that night. As Loren opened the show, and then when Tommy came on, and when they played together at the end, it was almost like the building itself began to seethe and heave with fervor. Magical!

After it was over and Tommy had moved on, people here at home talked about that show for months. So when we announced his return in 2006 the response was incredible. Since Jim Horsman, Loren and I were the founders of the Guitar League, (It was Jim's idea, so blame him.) we had decided to have the organization be the actual producer of the concerts. We wanted to expand Tommy's exposure in central New York and decided to produce shows in Syracuse, Rochester, and Ithaca. We had arranged for Tommy's group to stay in a tiny hotel in the beautiful resort village of Skaneateles, at the end of one of the region's FingerLakes. With Skaneateles as home base, if you connect the four locations with lines it makes something of a diamond shape. Following up on the Guitar League's baseball theme, we called it "The Bases Loaded Tour." That turned into an excellent promotional device and we "ran Tommy around the bases." (As you may start to suspect,

I was picking up on some of the concert promoter lingo.)

These regional concerts continued through 2008. Then The Roadmaster came back in 2012 to sell out shows in Rochester and Syracuse.

So it turned out to be a good and wise move. It got me off the road for one thing, and much more importantly, it introduced central New York to the genius of Tommy Emmanuel. To this day, I get a question every week or so, "When is Tommy coming back?" Because of his demeanor on stage, in local radio interviews, and in the "meet and greet" autograph line, people hereabouts think of Tommy as a friend. Tommy Emmanuel truly moves people that much.

Note: To find out about Guitar League, see appendix.

𝟕 𝓔 CGP

11

Loren at the RedHouse
January, 2005

Even as central New York winter days go, Saturday, January 22, was a blinger! After it started snowing heavily around midday, all it seemed to be able to do was get worse. Loren's first solo show was scheduled for this day, at the RedHouse performance space, in Syracuse. He and I planned to leave around 4:30 pm; he wanted to get there before the scheduled 5:30 load in to go over some business-end stuff with Heidi, the Red House event coordinator. As we drove east toward Syracuse, the snowfall rate kept getting deeper and higher. There was moderate traffic, even though there were no snowplows out and the roads were in really bad shape with just one lane where vehicles had blazed a trail. We wondered why no plows and still don't know. Fortunately Loren's van was a bit of a tank and plowed through.

We had been waiting all day for word that the show would be called off because the weather prognosis was "bad to worse", and there were cancellation announcements right and left on the local media. The airport closed and official proclamations of "no

unnecessary travel" were issued, but The Red House and
The Syracuse Symphony remained steadfast and held
the course. My bride's Syracuse Children's Chorus was
scheduled to perform with the Symphony. They both
chose to go on with the show, though we speculated on
whether there would be any audience to perform for in
either venue.

With encouragement from Scott Allyn, The Red House
music director (Scott's very words were, "Let's pack it
to the rafters!"), Loren had grossly oversold the 100-soul
capacity (figuring SRO) of the place with 162 paid
tickets. But what with the weather being as bad as it
was, we wondered if anyone would show up.

We arrived at the same time that Evan, the sound tech
from National Audio showed up. More on Evan and
NA later. We loaded in and of course Loren, the
featured performer, immediately grabbed a snow shovel
and went back out in the storm to clear walkways.

Loren's brothers, Paul and Brian, had arrived and loaded
in. Brian, the bass player, happened to have a rug in his
truck that he brought in to augment the one that was
already there and would be used to put Paul's drums on.
Set up and sound check went well, though Evan was a
tad taciturn. Was it shyness or did he just not give a
shit? We were to get a definitive answer during the
show.

As show time approached we stood around the dressing
rooms and chatted. The two-dozen bottles of tepid
water that I had insisted on were there, but the three

pounds of M&M's, red only, had apparently not arrived yet. There was also coffee and donuts. While lounging about we heard an unexpected sound: People were filtering in and by show time over 100 intrepid travelers had made the trek. I guess if you give central New Yorkers a challenge and a 4X4 SUV they will go anywhere, anytime.

Scott introduced Loren, with an anecdote relating the recent collision between Loren's son, LJ's, toy Tonka truck and Loren's brand new Maton guitar which resulted in a largish ding in the spruce top just under the low E string.

Loren opened with "Luttrell", the TE song that revisits Chet Atkins' birth town. He was not at all pleased with how it came out, but the audience loved it. This show would be something different for the audience, many of them loyal Loren fans, friends, and family; they were accustomed to seeing him play with his brothers or with Joe Whiting in a sideman role. This show would be mostly solo instrumentals.

He followed up his intro with "I'll Follow the Sun", "Old Fashioned Love Song", and "Imagine". He worked into his first vocal with some patter about the "other side" of Jerry Reed, versus *Smoky and the Bandit* and "Amos Moses" style. He did a wonderful version of the beautiful song, "A Thing Called Love", a Jerry Reed tune covered by everybody from Elvis to Roy Clark.

At that point he brought me on and we hit them with the Lyle Lovett song, "She's No Lady (She's My Wife)".

We did a pretty good job on it and the audience always eats that one up. We finished my slot with the "A Little Wiggle Room" cakewalk, which went well except for where it didn't, mostly the new ending I wrote on the spot and neglected to inform Loren about. But the crowd liked it. Several people mentioned it after the show.

Loren went on to put a blanket of hush over the place with his rendition of "Over the Rainbow", a truly moving experience. After this he got chatty and worked his way into Harry Chapin's "Six String Orchestra", a show and tell about trying to learn how to play the guitar. At the point he wishes for a bass and drums, his brothers filtered onto the stage and joined him. Very effective and of course the crowd loved it. Loren went on to say some nice things about his brothers and tell two anecdotes about his early exposure to fingerpicking, which involved "Freight Train". Then the three of them closed the first set out with "Freight Train" and "Caravan".

During the break, people were all over the stage and I expect that is when it happened. Anyway when he opened back up with "Classical Gas" his guitar was badly distorted, first in the monitor and then in the house mix. Thinking "batteries", I took his guitar while he grabbed mine. They are nearly identical. Back stage I put new batteries in as he started "Mr. Bojangles". Halfway through, Joe came on stage and finished the song vocally with him. I got his guitar back to him and it was then OK in the house, but the monitor continued to distort and was distorted throughout the rest of the show. Despite not so thinly veiled hints, good old Even Evan made the executive decision to let him live with it. Friend Loren was not happy about that. He would gladly have chatted the audience up while Evan switched out the monitor, but that was not to be. It is partly my fault because Loren tried to draw it to my attention hoping that I would put some pressure on Even Evan, but I thought he was still talking about the guitar, and didn't get what he wanted.

Evan's employer, National Audio, is a big sound company, based in Syracuse, and the scope of their business is indeed national. I have had a few unsatisfactory experiences with this company involving Swing Central, my wife Carol's vocal jazz band. NA does sound reinforcement gigs all over the country for major acts so they have to be good at what they do. The feeling I have come away with is that they, in the national touring self-image they have, see local acts as something to book just to keep their employees out of the bars at night and not really worthy of serious effort.

Loren and Joe then did Billy Joe Shaver's "Live Forever" and the Dillon tune, "Make You Feel My Love". I was hearing that last one for the first time ever and it is really beautiful.

Loren then played a new instrumental he had written commemorating the recent announcement that Mary was pregnant with their third child. It is called, "After the Shock Wears Off". Despite the kind of "gotcha" implication of the title it is really a smoldering, gorgeous ballad. He wrote it while Mary was still pregnant and after little Jack Diego Barrigar actually popped out, he reconsidered the song title. For his record and subsequent shows, it has been renamed, "Jack's Song."

At this point, time was becoming an issue and he skipped a country-picking medley that included "Cannon Ball Rag" and others. He was also scheduled to do "Please Come to Boston", a song that he just kills on, earlier in the set but for some reason skipped it. Probably because of the distortion glitch.

He sang the heartfelt Dan Seales song, "Everything That Glitters is not Gold" which the audience loved. Me too! I think I might add that to my show. Dammit, it is a solid country song with a unique story, filled with emotion.

As the night was winding down, Loren brought Brian back on and featured his bass playing on an arrangement of "Dance with Me". I wish you could see Brian play; everything coming out of his fingers plays across his face. He is one fine, fine player. Then Paul came back and they did the Jimmy Atkins' version of "Sweet Georgia Brown", wherein the three brothers demonstrate how they can mind-meld and play out of one brain. Using that Vulcan technique apparently makes it pretty easy to have three players hit every single syncopated kick as one.

Keeping Brian and Paul on stage Loren closed with his patriotic medley which included segments of "America the Beautiful", "I love the USA", "All My Trials", "Dixie Land" and "Battle Hymn of the Republic". I think I have them all and in the right order, but you will know when you get the CD. Even Evan allowed me to make a board recording. I don't know how well it came out but will get to editing it today.

I got a thank-you call from Loren, though God knows I should be thanking him for including me in the show. Other than that I have not heard much from him. I know sometimes that when you put a huge effort into something, there is a little let down that can wash over you when it is over. I don't know if he is experiencing that, but it would be understandable. He really ramped up to a peak for that night and now it's over. I guess the thing to do is start planning for the next big thing.

12

FPR with Loren
April, 2005

Fur Peace Ranch; St. Clair Road, (a hard left on a goat path off Rock Springs Road), Meigs County, southeastern Ohio and, Whoa! Hold it right there! You are already so far from the nearest interstate highway that a McDonalds is nothing but an unpleasant memory. You are in some of the most beautiful countryside that the midwestern United States has to offer. And what's more, it's spring! The coming forth! Why, on that beautiful April day at Fur Peace Ranch, Alison lay back in the hammock outside our cabins and assured Eddie and me that she could actually see leaves expanding out of their buds in the Maple tree over her head. And I think she probably could. Pretty young women can see things that the likes of Eddie and I never will.

This year, at the initial gathering of the Fur Peace Ranch season, there were five classes with 45 students, the most ever. But it was never crowded in the shower. That, by the way, is the measure that lets you know whether or not the attendance limits have been pushed.

I had convinced my excellent friend Loren Barrigar, a fine player and a "do right" man, to come to Fur Peace

Ranch with me. Loren is an incredible guitar player, by far the best I had ever encountered. I knew that he was deeply stirred by the magnitude of Tommy Emmanuel, and that closer contact with Tommy could only be a good thing. So my goal, by this time, was to simply try to put Loren and Tommy together on stage. I felt that it would be arrogant of me to think that I could make it happen, but maybe I could just get them together and "let it happen;" to just let the interaction of human chemistry do its work. It certainly went swiftly in that direction, but little did I suspect that a chance encounter at this workshop, with a guy from New Zealand, would change everything.

Loren and I surged out of hometown Elbridge at around 10 am on Thursday morning, with a bag full of enthusiasm. But wait! There's more! We also had a bag of Maureen's energy cookies, indispensable road trip provisions. Seems like before we even got all the talking done, we were in Marietta, Ohio looking for lodging. We wanted to drive into Fur Peace feeling nice and fresh on Friday morning. We stopped at a Hampton Inn but decided on a Motel 8, equally clean for half the price. Oh, and it was adjacent to a Shoney's, with the Hot Fudge Cake Sundaes and all. That might have influenced our decision in some small measure.

We got the guitars and bags out of the truck, but I left the energy cookies and all the rest of our stuff in the back of the truck. I wanted to use it as bait in order to try out my new pickup truck security system that Dougie, from over to the Ace Hardware, and I had invented. My truck had the top-of-the-line cap on it, but a baby, or even a small raccoon, could break it open. I went back to the cap company to talk about how they would recommend that I make it more secure, and they basically said, "Huh?" But Doug and I came up with a good solution. I, of course, did all the thinking, and Dougie assembled the parts, but we got 'er done. Worked well too. I should say that Doug is a former English student of mine. 7th grade. To this day, he thinks that I was his math teacher. That is a statement about something, but I have never been able to figure out quite what. He would know better if he could see how I try to balance my check book.

We settled in, phoned home, played a bit, but mostly talked about Tommy Emmanuel. Oh yeah, we talked about our picker buddy, Geoff Richard, too. Pretty cool, when he's not around, but better when he is there to hear it!

I had always thought that Tommy's concert in Old Church, the previous year in Portland, was the best I had ever seen, but after Fur Peace I can't say that anymore. Tommy never fails to catch me unawares. Something he said in one of the classes at Fur Peace explains it, I think. He said that he would be angry if he did not do something to improve his playing, and himself, each and every day. Given that, I decided that what I had always thought was momentary inspiration in these incredible concert performances, is really more calculated and part of a long-range plan. Through practice, growth, and design, Tommy just keeps getting better and better.

So, after driving well out of civilization as we know it, and finally arriving at the Fur Peace Ranch, Loren and I were reeled in and warmly welcomed by Vanessa, Jorma's wife who is sort of the CEO of Fur Peace. Jorma handles teaching, playing guitar, and running motorcycles around southeastern Ohio, while Vanessa keeps the whole FPR scene ticking along smoothly and efficiently. She is great, just like all the rest of the Fur Peace experience.

When we pulled in, Tommy was sitting on a porch, picking, and he had gathered a crowd like always. I introduced Loren to everyone, and then it all becomes a four day blur. I know we soon went to the dining hall and gorged on the terrific food. The rest of the evening was spent shooting the bull with people we knew and people we had just met, and groovin' on Tommy's playing. The watchword was relaxation and picking! Oh, and then some more picking!

One of the players who had come to be in Tommy's group was a young guy from New Zealand, Mark Mazengarb. He was an exchange student at North Carolina State, finishing his degree in classical guitar. It was obvious that he was a really good player, but he did not have much experience playing Travis style. Loren and I gravitated toward him and struck up a friendship right off the bat.

When the 10 of us met the next morning for the first seminar with Tommy, he played a bit and then asked each of us to play something, so that he could gauge our ability and tailor his workshop accordingly. I honestly have no idea what I played then, except that it was unremarkable. I was too stoked by Loren and Tommy being in the same room together, with guitars in their hands. Loren caught Tommy's attention early on, and in subsequent sessions, he frequently used Loren to demonstrate what he was teaching. Mark was just sort of lookin' and cookin' in the background among the other students, taking it all in. Who knew what was to come of this?

Tommy decided to teach us how to play "Borsalino," the theme song from a 1970's gangster movie. We were to play it as a group, at the Saturday night student concert at Fur Peace Station, Jorma's new performance hall. We worked hard at it and were ready for the show in the theater. It is a beautifully designed room with superb acoustics. People come from Columbus and other Ohio locations to hear shows at Fur Peace Station.

Before the group rendition of "Borsalino," We each had a chance to do a solo thing. I did some little bailout song that I do not even remember now. It was just something that I could get through in front of two of the world's greatest guitar players. Funny thing though, it went over pretty well. Wish I could remember what it was! If you ask Geoff Richard, he will tell you that it was "The Hesitation Waltz."

When it was Loren's turn, he played "Dance with Me." Tommy and Jorma were standing off stage to the right. In the off stage shadows, I saw them simply nod to each other once when Loren played. Jorma's gold tooth glinted from the stage lights. I think they liked it.

Tommy's students played our "Borsalino" number, complete with finger twirl visual at the end, and brought the house down! It was such a very cool thing to be a part of!

We students all had a lot of bonding and mutual enjoyment, understanding where we all were coming from with our playing. We inhaled the beautiful nervous tension involved in playing in front of the world's best and grew because of it.

Meanwhile, Mark Mazengarb told us that he was headed back to North Carolina State and from there was going to Toronto to visit friends of his parents. I informed him that he could not get to Toronto without going through Syracuse, so we made plans for him to stop and spend a few days with us on his way through. That was the start of it all, with him and Loren. Loren was in the midst of his Tommy epiphany, having been a child prodigy, then a never-need-to-practice local guitarist, to a player who suddenly saw new challenges and new goals to strive for. Mark started soaking up Loren's licks and improving on them. When he came back from New Zealand a couple years later they were ready to begin putting together the International Guitar Duo, which would become such a presence in the fingerstyle guitar world.

When the weekend at FPR was all said and done, Loren and I drove home; we were on autopilot, caused by adrenalin overload and sleep deprivation. We pretty much limped back into Elbridge. But not without our last 20 miles of reinforcement from Ronnie Milsap's *Stranger Things Have Happened,* on the stereo.

Though our homes are about a 7 iron apart in the little village of Elbridge, NY, (well, a maybe 3 wood for him) I don't think I talked to Loren for about a week after we got home; we had no words to share for awhile. The things we brought home with us just had to marinate for a time. Strange, but that's how it was.

Note: Since 2005, Loren and Mark, The International Guitar Duo, has performed all over the U.S. and Europe. After that first encounter at FPR, the two players met informally for a couple years and then played together at the Chet Atkins Appreciation Society convention in Nashville. There was so much positive excitement for their playing there, that they decided to try to make a go of it as a touring act. This implies a commitment of tons of rehearsal time, business planning, investment, and traveling. Mark obtained his U.S. work visa and moved here, though he returns to New Zealand periodically. To date the Loren and Mark duo has toured extensively in the U.S., twice in Europe, and will be in New Zealand this fall. Next year will find them back in New Zealand, Europe and even in Russia. They never forget their roots though, and always credit Tommy for bringing them together and for the inspiration that keeps them fresh. They open shows for Tommy now and then as well. Follow their journey at
http://www.lorenandmark.com

7 ℰ CGP

Conclusion

It is July, 2013, shortly after I returned from CAAS. Tommy was not there this year, because he can't be everywhere. I had a good time at CAAS, as usual, reconnecting with old friends, and, of course, enjoying the music of Loren and Mark and all the other wonderful players from all over the world.

So it occurred to me while coming back from CAAS this year that it is high time that I wrote the piece that would signal the end of my Tommy Emmanuel book. This is it. It does not mean that there is an end to anything else; just that I am going to wrap up this journal and finally get it out to you all. I want to share the exciting ride that I have been privileged to enjoy with Tommy Emmanuel.

Oh wait! I promised to tell you about the Little Dickie thing. Tommy and Liz and I were walking down the street in Skaneateles one afternoon and I don't know how it came up, but I told them that I was named after my uncle, Dick Clark. I told them that I was not aware of any actual insecurities that I might have, but if I did have any, it was probably because when I was a kid, my uncle was called, "Big Dick" and I was called, "Little Dick." There you have it; to Tommy, I have been Little

Dickie since that day.

This actual narrative ends in 2005, when I stopped following TE and he started coming to us here in central New York. However there are several other chronicles in a future book that you may find interesting and informative.

It is hard to find a way to conclude my writing about a person who changed my life as profoundly as Tommy Emmanuel did. So I will just do it quickly and simply:

Tommy told me that he learned early on that his guitar playing made people happy; he said that he was in the "happiness business." Tommy, thank you for being the person that you are as you travel this world, bringing happiness wherever you go. As the happiness spirit moves through Chet Atkins to you, you are an incomparable gift to us all.

Acknowledgments

Writing this book was way too much fun! Sometimes I think I amuse myself almost as much as Geoff Richard does. But on the more serious side, I want to thank some people without whom this thing could never have happened.

My fine friend, Don A. Singletary is a teacher and an author, among many other accomplishments. His speciality is the art of self-publishing. Without his help and encouragement, and a bit of prodding, you would not be reading this.

Many thanks to Trish Nelson and Carol Bryant for their technical help in getting this text ready for publishing. Now that the book is finished, they can go back to what they do best: Shopping!

Thanks to Loren Barrigar for riding shotgun on several of my Tommy related journeys. He has been my "guitar buddy" for a long time.

Gotta thank Mark Mazengarb for two things: keeping me inspired by his incessant practicing in my living room, and for asking me every day for the last several weeks, "So, is the book finished yet?"

I have used Geoff Richard as a foil in several places in this book. The truth is that back at that first Fur Peace Ranch weekend, he encouraged me to approach Tommy with the demo of the words I had written for "Those Who Wait", and in the aftermath of that singular incident, he counseled me to not over-react, but just to wait and see. Thanks Geoff, you were right. It's all good.

And of course, thanks to the Roadmaster, Tommy Emmanuel, without whom my scatter-gun approach to life would not have achieved the focus I have enjoyed since July 2002.

Appendix

Guitar Frenzy Itinerary

Friday, Jul 30: UNITED AIRLINES, UA 1805
From: SYRACUSE, NY (SYR) Departs: 7:30am
To: PHILADELPHIA, PA (PHL) Arrives: 8:45am

Friday, Jul 30: UNITED AIRLINES, UA 3766
From: PHILADELPHIA, PA (PHL) Departs:10:10am
To: NEWPORT NEWS, VA (PHF) Arrives: 11:20am

Attend Tommy Fest East for three days with Tommy and Stephen Bennett at the Yoder Barn.

Monday, Aug 2: DELTA AIR LINES INC, DL 4132
From: NEWPORT NEWS, VA (PHF) Departs: 5:30am
To: ATLANTA, GA (ATL) Arrives: 7:18am

Monday, Aug 2: DELTA AIR LINES INC, DL 1277
From: ATLANTA, GA (ATL) Departs: 8:30am
To: PORTLAND OR, OR (PDX) Arrives: 10:33am

Attend Accent on Music seminar at Lewis and Clark College for one week, with Tommy, John Knowles and Mark Hanson.

Now I will start for home and get there five airports later! Jet Lag Du Jour

Sunday, Aug 8: DELTA AIR LINES INC, DL 1676
From: PORTLAND OR, OR (PDX) Departs: 8:30am
To: ATLANTA, GA (ATL) Arrives: 4:11pm

Sunday, Aug 8: DELTA AIR LINES INC, DL 4318
From: ATLANTA, GA (ATL) Departs: 5:00pm
To: NEWPORT NEWS, VA (PHF) Arrives: 6:45pm

Sunday, Aug 8: UNITED AIRLINES, UA 3765
From: NEWPORT NEWS, VA (PHF) Departs: 7:40pm
To: PHILADELPHIA, PA (PHL)Arrives:8:50pm

Sunday, Aug 8: UNITED AIRLINES, UA 3902
From: PHILADELPHIA, PA (PHL) Departs: 10:20pm
To: SYRACUSE, NY (SYR) Arrives: 11:31pm

Home again, home again, jiggedy jig! (Whew!)

7 ℰ CGP

About Being Ready

After the general workshop with more than 40 players in Elizabethtown, I thought I needed to wait until I was "ready" before I enrolled in a more personalized seminar, such as Fur Peace Ranch, where it is Tommy and just 10 students. Since then, I have learned that if you adhere to that philosophy and wait "until you are ready," ready to go to a workshop, ready to play at an open mike, ready to get your first gig, then none of those things will ever happen.

The guitar, according to Andrés Segovia, is the easiest instrument to play poorly, and the hardest to play well. There is not and never will be a moment with this instrument when you are at your "best" and totally ready to show your stuff. That is because it is not your stuff! It belongs totally to the guitar. And your "best" is always waiting for you somewhere up the fretboard. The guitar deviously whispers in your ear, "You can really do better with me if you work a little longer and work a little harder, and wait until you are ready."

Instead, listen to your guitar when it yells, "C'mon, let's

do it! Into the deep end of the pool! If you crash and burn, you will be better next time because of it." I know that this is true because Tommy told me so.

7 ℰ CGP

Guitar League

Here is what Guitar League is all about:
- The Guitar League meets once a month in Syracuse, NY, and was founded by three local players: Jim Horsman, Loren Barrigar, and myself.

- We had our first meeting in April 2005 with 18 players in a room. We currently have more than 120 members and we average 75 to 90 people per meeting. About 85% of our members are living room guitarists; about 10% play out at least occasionally, with several playing regularly. A few are full-time professional musicians.

- Monthly meetings have two distinct segments: We start off each meeting with a main presenter, someone who has something to share with guitar players of all levels. In the past we have had a luthier talk to us about guitar set up and maintenance. Other meetings have featured players who make a living with their guitars. One presentation featured the business side of playing out. In an October meeting we had a seminar on mapping the fretboard. A recent meeting was with a nationally known builder of resonator guitars, and another time, a musician/psychologist discussed performance anxiety.

• Following the main presentation, we move to the second segment. We break off into the three leagues Rookies, Minors, and Majors. There is a presentation in each that is appropriate to that level. Each month's Rookie presentation, for example, is self-contained and does not build on the previous month, like a series of lessons would. So you can miss a month and not be lost. They are not guitar lessons; they are workshop-type presentations. Folks can take content home from each session that will help make them better players.

• Often at the end of the second segment we save time for a couple people in that league to play a song for the group if they choose. There is never any pressure for anyone to play, though there is a lot of positive encouragement for those who do.

• Players gather during and after the meetings to swap licks and play informally for each other.

• The first meeting is always free. From then on a person can join by paying yearly membership dues or pay on a "per meeting" basis.

- The Guitar League also produces concerts for the membership and the public. We kicked off the series in April 2005 by bringing Tommy Emmanuel to two sold out shows in Syracuse. Harp guitarist, Stephen Bennett, and Chet Atkins' associate and Grammy winner, John Knowles did concerts and workshops earlier in 2006. In 2007, we had what we call "Bases Loaded Tours" with Stephen Bennett, Laurence Juber, and Tommy Emmanuel. We scheduled the performer for concerts and workshops in three nearby cities: Syracuse, Rochester, and Ithaca. We run them around the bases, with their hotel in a nearby resort village, being home plate. We continue to produce 2 or 3 concerts per year.

- We have a website and also use Facebook to provide information about Guitar League.

Member also get:

- Substantially reduced pricing on concert tickets and workshops. (This is a very popular feature. Go fig.)
- Free link to their website or Facebook page from the GL website
- Free listing of gigs on the website forum
- Discounts at local music retailers

7 E CGP

Tommy Emmanuel: Roadmaster

In 2007, Loren discovered the incredible cars, Buick Roadmaster Estate Wagons. You know, like station wagons with the wood on the sides. They were made from 1992 through 1996. We think they are a mistake made by GM engineers back then because the engines are so reliable and rarely break. Of course, you have the minor attrition with wear and tear, and replacement of alternators, brakes, power steering pumps and the like, and to be true, the transmissions can be dicey. But the engines are Corvette LT-1 motors and are not only reliable and long lived, but also weirdly efficient, getting much higher mileage that you would expect with a boat like the Estate Wagon.

For musicians, they are a luxury. After years and years of crawling in and out of the dark caves of pickup trucks, or unlacing the equipment from the trunks and back seats of the cars we used to drive to gigs, to be able to transport the music equipment in a vehicle like this is bliss. It is so easy to load in and load out; the back seat and the rear facing seat in the way-back, both fold down to create a huge deck. With the back doors and tailgate, you then have three points of entry and total accessibility for getting the gear in and out. Also, it doesn't hurt that the tailgate opens two ways for your load in/load out convenience. It can be lowered flat like most tailgates, or opened out to the side like a regular door. Ah, good old American engineering!

Plus a "woody" has that kind of cool that makes everybody smile to see one. The car is reliable, rides like a cloud down the road and is fun to drive. It has a sweet spot when you get it out on the interstate at around 73 mph. After you merge into traffic, it seems to grab a big gulp of air and settle into an easy rolling rhythm that uses a minimum of gas and makes you feel good about being on the road again.

Loren always thought of Tommy as "The Roadmaster" because of his incredible tour schedule of over 300 concerts per year!

Oh, one more thing: With the big old 8 cylinder Corvette engine, it is fun to be at a traffic light when a young blood pulls up beside you in his dad's Honda. He looks over at you and you can see the "old fart in an old car" look come across his face. Then the light changes and all he sees is the tail lights of your old fart car--- soooooo gone!

7E CGP

Those Who Wait

© Richard Ward, 2004

The children are sleeping,
You sit and you stare at the phone,
He said he would call you,
You'll know if it rings, it's got to be him, he said he would call.

You know what you'll tell him,
That everything's fine here at home,
You'll say what you know you should,
So it's not so hard, so you can go on.

Chorus:
'Till he comes home your life's on hold, and so empty,
The rules all change when you're alone,
There's nothing more to say,
It's just all wrong when he's away,
That's how it is for those who wait.

His mother came over,
She said she would stay with the kids,
You guess you should let her,
And get out of this house, and get something to do,
But what if he calls?

It's making you crazy,

You want him to be here at home,
You need to be near him,
But you'll just hang on, what else can you do.

Chorus, Instrumental

There's nothing more to say,
It's just all wrong when he's away,
That's how it is for those who wait.
That's how it is for those who wait.

Note: Just change the "he/him" pronouns to make it the woman who is away.

7 𝓔 CGP

Letter to Christine Yoder After My Unfortunate Experience in Newport News

101 Meadow Drive
Elbridge, New York, 13060

Ms. Christine Yoder
660 Hamilton Drive
Newport News, Virginia, 23602

Dear Christine,
My name is Dick Ward. I'm the guy that was at the Tommy Emmanuel/Stephen Bennett concert way early on Friday, July 30, and helped load the flowers into the van before you opened the doors for the concert. I also am the one who got you to give those three ladies a tour of the Barn; sorry about that!

I came to the Hampton Inn directly from the airport by cab and wanted to tell you about my experience there. I enjoyed the Friday night concert but woke up Saturday morning with a heart related medical situation. The staff at the hotel was incredible in my time of need! It was not an emergency so I did not require an ambulance but I did need to get to the hospital. They had the shuttle driver take me and assured me that I did not have to worry about my guitar or other things in my room. I can't remember the driver's name (I hate it when I do that.) but he was reluctant to just drop me off and leave me. I assured him that I would be fine, expecting that I would be treated and released that afternoon. He told me to just call anytime and he would come and pick me up.

I ended up staying at the Riverside medical facility and they kept me overnight, finally releasing me Sunday afternoon. The Hampton Inn shuttle driver was there to pick me up when I was discharged. So here I was, alone in an unfamiliar city and in trouble. I am so impressed with the hotel staff's level of caring and attention to my needs. I hope that you will convey my thanks to them. I think it will be more meaningful coming from you than if I just write a letter to the hotel.

Unfortunately I missed the entire weekend. I got to the Yoder Barn in time for the last half hour of Stephen Bennett's workshop on Sunday and was unable to go to the Sunday night concert. I was too tired from the hospital treatment, and had to catch a 5:30 am flight on Monday.

I hope to get to all the Tommy Fest East events next year.
Thanks,

Dick Ward

7 E CGP

Sand A440

$\mathcal{TE}$ CGP

EBG808TE, with CGP inlay on neck

7 ℰ CGP
EBG808 Artist

Though it is hard to see here, the binding on this guitar is Queen's Land Maple, not plastic.

Made in the USA
Charleston, SC
13 February 2014